Soutache
& Bead
Embroidery

Amee K. Sweet-McNamara

KB

KALMBACH BOOKS

This book is dedicated to my mother, Donna.

Though I have long since come to understand that her particular brand of poise, patience, and strength is something to which I have not the faintest hope of ever aspiring, she nevertheless inspires me. And so, I continue—with lurching, graceless tenacity—to try.

Kalmbach Books
21027 Crossroads Circle
Waukesha, Wisconsin 53186
www.Kalmbach.com/Books

Published in 2014
18 17 16 15 14   1 2 3 4 5

Manufactured in the United States of America

ISBN: 978-0-87116-750-7
EISBN: 978-1-62700-088-8

Editor: Erica Swanson
Art Director: Lisa Bergman
Technical Editor: Jane Danley Cruz
Layout Designer: Tom Ford
Photographer: James Forbes

Publisher's Cataloging-in-Publication Data
Sweet-McNamara, Amee K.
   Soutache & bead embroidery / Amee K. Sweet-McNamara.

   p. : col. ill. ; cm.

   Issued also as an ebook.
   ISBN: 978-0-87116-750-7

   1. Bead embroidery—Handbooks, manuals, etc. 2. Braid—Handbooks, manuals, etc. 3. Jewelry making—Handbooks, manuals, etc. 4. Beadwork—Handbooks, manuals, etc. I. Title. II. Title: Soutache and bead embroidery

TT860 .S94 2014
745.594/2

CONTENTS

Foreword

By deciding to purchase this book, you have placed yourself in the very capable hands of Amee K. Sweet-McNamara. When I think of Amee, I'm reminded of a song from "A Chorus Line," "I Can Do That." As a juried member of the League of New Hampshire Craftsmen, an accomplished painter, designer, writer, photographer, teacher, techno whiz, and cook, there is nothing that Amee is not able to do. Readers and students of her classes will be impressed by her patient attention to detail, a hallmark of her teaching style.

We met when my husband and I were house-hunting in December of 2002. Our search led us to look at the Victorian neighboring Amee and her husband's home. When she saw us coming up the walkway, she popped her head out the door, introduced herself, and asked us in for tea. When we entered their home, we were embraced by color. Rooms were painted in warm rich hues—one a deep saturated blue with touches of lime green, another, a golden orange yellow, another, a martini olive green, and yet another, a ruby slipper red. The palette was bold, fearless, and inviting—just like Amee herself.

As we sat around the table, we began the relationship that would grow and evolve into the friendship and artistic collaboration we enjoy today. At the time, Amee and her husband had taken up skydiving. (In hindsight, she could have easily called her business "Amee Jumps from Airplanes.") We talked about our work, hers as a kitchen and bath designer, and mine as a jeweler who uses "upcycled" elements. As a fiber artist, Amee had a studio filled with fabric where she made woven hats and purses from ribbon and trim. She gave me a "Welcome, Neighbor" hat and purse she had made. I reciprocated with a necklace I had made from an antique chandelier crystal.

When we bought the house next door, I went about selecting paint colors. Knowing I could rely on Amee's decisive and unerring eye, I asked her to help me to decide between the darker or lighter versions of a color from a Benjamin Moore paint swatch I had picked for the kitchen. "That one, Semolina," she said, with no hesitation. A few years later, we were having dinner at her house and I commented that I had always meant to ask what that golden orange yellow color in her dining room was. She paused then said, "Semolina." She explained that she never told me because she wanted me to make the color my own without feeling as if I had copied her.

Amee had become fascinated with bead embroidery. She started to create elaborate beaded and fringed neckpieces. The first one she made, "Koala Face," uses polymer clay and seed beads. The scale is quite large, but you can see it reflected in her smaller scaled, highly detailed soutache and bead embroidery of today. I wanted to combine my love of found objects like telephone wire, paint swatches, and vintage buttons with Amee's love of textiles and ornamentation, so we started a creative back-and-forth. I'd give her a broken earring and she'd make it into the center-piece of a soutache embroidered component, which I would use as an element in a piece of jewelry I designed. She die-cut and stitched a button onto the paint swatch I had given her. Anything I threw Amee's way, like the heroine in Rumpelstiltskin, she'd spin into gold.

There has always been the excitement that goes back and forth between us as we build and create our jewelry. "Can I come over and show you what I made?" "I got this great idea and I want you to see it!" "Could you use these vintage pink pearl cabs I found?" "I'm at a sticking point with this design; could you take a look at it and tell me what it needs?" "You usually go for earthy and monochromatic. You know what will really make it pop? Semolina!"

Amee will say she considers me to be her mentor and that she was motivated to create her own jewelry business after seeing mine. Although I've shared my knowledge, experience, and materials with her, the truth is that we mentor each other. Our friendship and collaborations use the language of color, texture, and design. She has inspired me by finding her own voice as an artist, her commitment to excellence, her gratitude, her nonstop creativity, and her drive to constantly develop and refine her craft.

Victoria Tane, Nashua, NH
January, 2013

Introduction

For over 5,000 years, beads have been used to create art and adornment. Beads themselves come in an endless variety of materials, shapes, sizes, and colors, and have been strung, woven, loomed, knitted and embroidered into everything from jewelry to place mats to key chains. And based on the huge number of craft books currently available—each taking traditional techniques one step further with a new stitch, pattern, or project—it would seem that people's curiosity and hunger for new ways of creating with these oddly addictive particles of glass, shell, wood, and stone is equally infinite.

But what if there was a brand-new way of working with beads? A craft that was fundamentally simple to learn and required no expensive equipment or materials but which—like so many beading techniques—was virtually unlimited in its creative possibilities?

While simply a very new way of working with very old materials, the results of soutache and bead embroidery—curving, organic shapes and rich textural combinations—absolutely demand further exploration. Personally, I find that every piece I make kindles a little spark, another idea, another concept jostling against a dozen others all clamoring to be developed. So, whether you are a bead enthusiast, fiber artist, or jewelry maker, I am confident that this technique will ignite your imagination as well and you too will become fascinated, hooked, and ensnared.

There are 18 projects in this book and—while I encourage you to work on the projects you find most exciting—it is important to understand that the chapters and projects therein are laid out to teach a new skill in each project and provide greater challenges as you go. In Chapter 1, the projects are more broken down with a greater level of detail. In Chapter 2, the projects get more challenging and the instructions are written with the assumption that you've already mastered much of Chapter 1. Chapter 3 provides even more exciting projects, and the instructions will be focused on the newest techniques.

Can you skip around in this book? Of course you can! Just be prepared for the fact that you may need to backtrack now and again to pick up something you may have missed. Common techniques are called out in boldface type so, if you can't quite remember how to do something, you can quickly take a peek back at the Basic Techniques section, which is arranged alphabetically for easy reference.

Do you have to follow the instructions precisely? No, of course not! What if you have a slightly different bead? What if you want to use alternate colors? I encourage you to play! Experiment! Color outside the lines! Run with scissors! For me, beadwork is a joy. I simply want to share my knowledge and ideas with you in a way that will inspire you to develop your own techniques that resonate with your own artistic voice and illuminate the Spirit of the Maker within you.

SUPPLIES

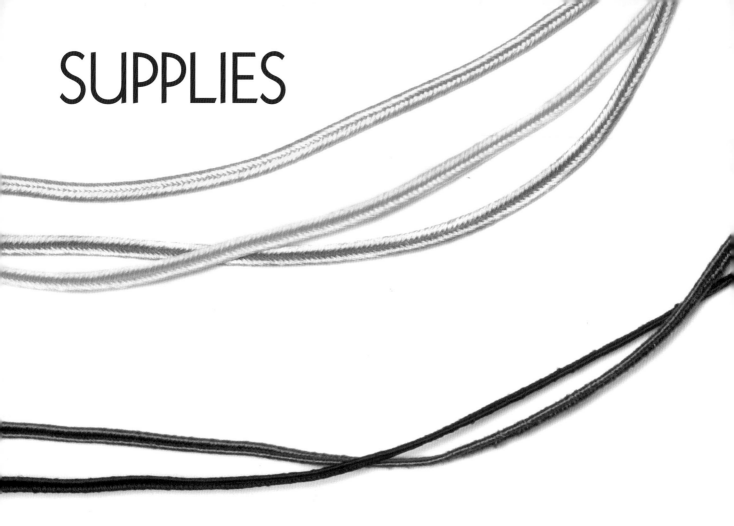

Soutache

Soutache is braid made up of fine fibers wrapped figure-eight style around two core cords. Also commonly referred to as Russia braid, soutache is one of the basic elements used in passementerie—the French art of textile embellishment. This craft includes tassel-making, upholstery enhancements such as gimp and fringe, as well as clothing decoration, such as the swirling braids seen on band and military uniforms. Soutache can be made of silk, polyester, rayon,

> Before you begin, you'll need a list of materials and tools, along with a discussion of basic soutache and bead embroidery techniques. You can also refer back to these pages when you need a refresher as you work on the projects.

or metallized fibers (like Lurex), or any combination thereof, and it is widely available in both ⅛" and ¼". In this book, I use the ⅛" variety, and even within this seemingly narrow world, there are many variations of width, thickness, sheen, and drape. These are very general categories:

Imported: Frequently made in Thailand, imported soutache is usually made of polyester and is shiny, thick, and wide. The fibers are loosely braided, so it frays more at the cut ends, and it is susceptible to snagging. Its beefier dimensions, however, make it easier for a beginner to manipulate, and it works better with larger beads. Remember to cut your imported soutache pieces extra-long to avoid having to fight with frayed ends.

Domestic: Domestic soutache runs the gamut in terms of sheen and

drape but, in general, it is slightly narrower, thinner, and more tightly braided. These qualities allow for more delicate, detailed work incorporating smaller beads.

Metallic: Metallics can be smooth or textured and can add tremendous sparkle to a piece. Remember to wriggle or twist your needle if you encounter resistance when using metallic soutache, since forcing your needle through will break the fine metallic fibers and cause burrs.

The "rib" of the soutache refers to the indented line running the length of both sides of the braid. The "grain" refers to the direction in which the fibers of the braid are oriented.

BeadSmith brand jewelry soutache: This product is the first line of soutache developed especially for

jewelry-makers, with much attention paid to consistency of width, thickness, and drape. Using this brand of domestic soutache eliminates a lot of headaches. The braid is very tight, so there is less fraying, and the finished work has a wonderful density that is less apt to snag. The color selection includes solids, stripes, and metallics, all designed to work together.

Other Materials

Beads: Beads may or may not serve as a focal point, but they always act as a support or armature for the soutache. You'll use all kinds of beads in your work, including seed beads in sizes ranging from 15° to 6° and a selection of 3–8mm round, oval, cube, and bicone shapes. Barrels, teardrops, and double-cones that are 5–12mm work well, too. Flat beads like lentils, diamonds, and marquise shapes can be tricky, since they often spin around inside the soutache as you work, but larger versions of these shapes can be stitched to a foundation and incorporated much like a cabochon. Shapes with a concave edge, like crescent, dogbone, kidney, or bamboo shapes, do not work well.

Ear wires: Choose ear wires on which the "loop" part of the ear wire is in the same plane as the "hook" part. This will allow the finished earring to hang perpendicular to the ear wire, and a little twist with a pair of pliers can gently angle the work slightly toward the front. (If the earring loop hangs parallel to the ear wire hook, earrings will often stick out too much on the wearer's head and/or get caught behind her jaw.)

Jump rings: I use 6mm soldered jump rings almost exclusively. You can use cut jump rings, but stitches often get caught in or slide through the opening.

Headpins and eye pins: Use these for adding dangles to finished work.

Toggles and clasps: Closures for your necklaces and soft bracelets are available in a wide variety of sizes, styles, and finishes. Choose findings that enhance your finished work.

Crimp tubes and covers: I like crimp tubes (instead of crimp beads) because they have more surface contact with the beading wire, giving the finished work more security. Check the label on your beading wire for the recommended size crimp tube. Crimp covers that are 3mm hide the crimp for a professional finish.

Cuff blanks: Brass cuff blanks come in a variety of shapes and sizes.

SUPPLIES

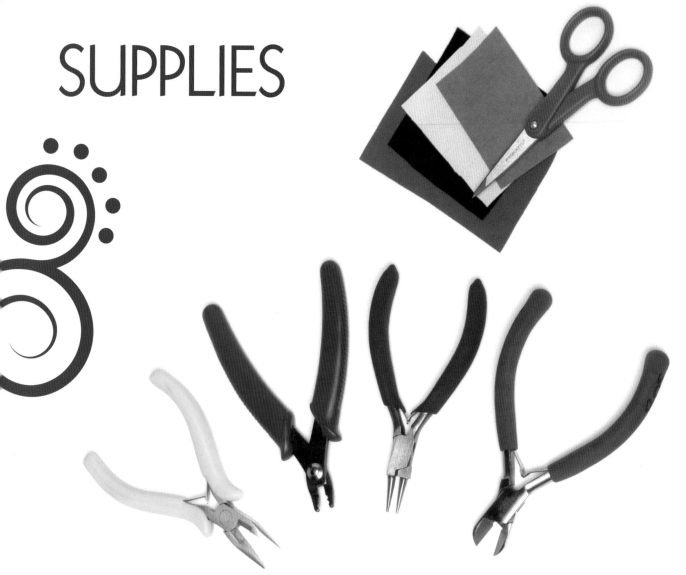

Think of the surface of the cuff as a canvas, and select the size that will best fit the work.

Beading foundation: My two favorite beading foundations are Lacy's Stiff Stuff and Nicole's Bead Backing. Lacy's is slightly lighter and more flexible, and can be dyed or colored with a permanent marker. Nicole's is a bit heavier and is available in an assortment of rich, vibrant colors.

Beading wire: For stringing, I recommend a 49-strand wire, such as Beadalon or Accuflex. Choose the size that offers the degree of drape that is appropriate for your project—thicker wire (.018) for larger pieces with heavy beads, thinner wire (.024) for lighter work with small beads.

Clothespins: Spring-loaded clothespins are a great way to hold things in place while gluing.

Darning needle: I use darning needles for adjusting the final shape of a piece, for poking errant strands of beading wire or thread into place, and even for getting glue exactly where I want it. Because they're made of steel, they can easily be wiped or scraped clean.

Drafter's inking template: Inking templates allow you to trace basic shapes such as circles, squares, and ellipses quickly and accurately. You can find them at most large office supply stores.

Fusible webbing: When I want to bring Ultrasuede or another fabric to the forefront, I use Mistyfuse brand fusible webbing to bond my fabric to a beading foundation. This eliminates the possibility of bleed-through from glue and adds no bulk.

Glue: I really only use one kind of glue: api brand Crafter's Pick washable fabric glue. It is nontoxic, water-soluble, and behaves like the good old-fashioned white glue we all used in school. Unlike some of the heavy-duty jewelry glues, it remains flexible after it dries so you can still run a needle through it. After about two weeks, it's fully cured and can actually be hand-washed with soap and water (an important feature for finished work that is essentially a textile).

Thread: Use a good-quality beading thread and select a color that coordinates with your design, since it will show on the back of the work. I like

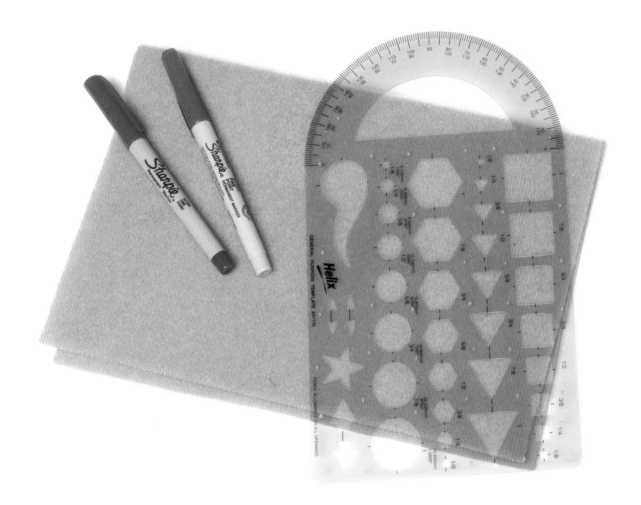

Nymo brand thread, size B, and I typically work with a 36" length.

Ultrasuede: For my backing, I use Ultrasuede Soft, the medium-weight version of the product. It's available in a fabulous rainbow of colors that will enhance your design.

Tools

Flush cutters: Use these for cutting headpins down to size and snipping away those pesky little ends of beading wire.

Iron: Use a regular household steam iron to bond your fabrics together.

Markers: Use Sharpie-brand permanent makers to dye Lacy's Stiff Stuff without the mess. Just color the piece you need with a color-coordinated marker and wait a minute or so to make sure it's dry.

Needles: I use size #10 long beading needles for pretty much everything. If I'm working with tiny 15º seed beads, I might switch to a size #12.

Pliers: Crimping pliers are used to flatten and fold crimp tubes; be sure to use the right-sized pliers for the tubes you're using. Keep at least two pairs of flatnose pliers on hand. They can be used to tug a needle through a resistant spot or open and close findings without marring them. Use looping pliers to make centered loops in dangles and bead-chain links. You can use roundnose pliers, but if you want to make a lot of bead chain, I really recommend purchasing a pair of bail-making or 6-in-1 looping pliers. The noses of these types of pliers are non-tapered, cylindrical shapes, allowing you to select a loop size and get exactly the same size loop every time.

Scissors: Use one pair of large, fabric-cutting scissors and a smaller pair of craft or embroidery scissors, which have very sharp points designed for cutting into small corners. A good pair of cuticle scissors can give you great control when trimming the backing from negative spaces.

Working space: A bead blanket is inexpensive and keeps your beads from rolling around. Cut it down to the size of a cookie sheet.

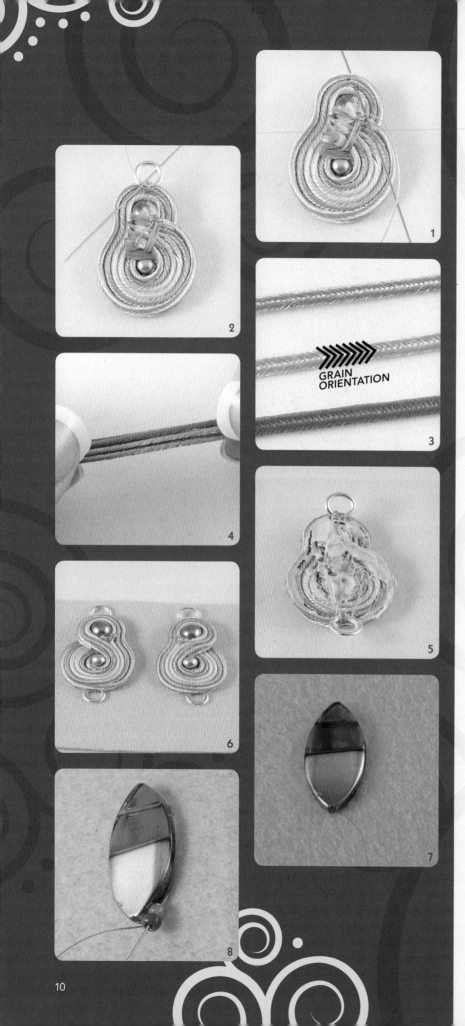

As you are working through the projects, basic techniques will be noted in **boldface type**. Most will quickly become second nature to you, but you can return to this section for a quick recap, if necessary. Techniques are listed in alphabetical order for easy reference as you work.

Add a jump ring

Working from the back of the work, sew through two outermost braids where you want your finding to be attached **(photo 1)**. Pick up a 6mm jump ring and make three or four **whip stitches** to secure the jump ring behind the edge of the work **(photo 2)**. **Bury the thread** in the back of the work, and trim.

Align and stack

Orient each length of soutache so the grain of the braid is pointed in the same direction **(photo 3)**. Stack the soutache, one piece on top of the other, from bottom to top. Hold from the outer edges to keep the stack aligned **(photo 4)**.

Apply backing

Apply a dab of glue to the back of the work. Use your finger, a darning needle, or a toothpick to spread glue just to the edges of the work **(photo 5)**. Use glue sparingly over the beads so it does not ooze through to the front of the work. Place the glued shape on the wrong side of a piece of Ultrasuede, and let dry completely **(photo 6)**.

Backstitch

One of the basic stitches used in bead embroidery, backstitch is used to lay down a line of two beads at a time, often in a curving path.

A. Sew up from the bottom of the beading foundation. Pick up two beads **(photo 7)**. Sew down through the beading foundation just barely beyond the end of the second bead **(photo 8)**.

B. Sew back up through the beading foundation so the thread is exiting just behind the second bead **(photo 9)**. Sew through the second bead, and pick up two beads.

QUES

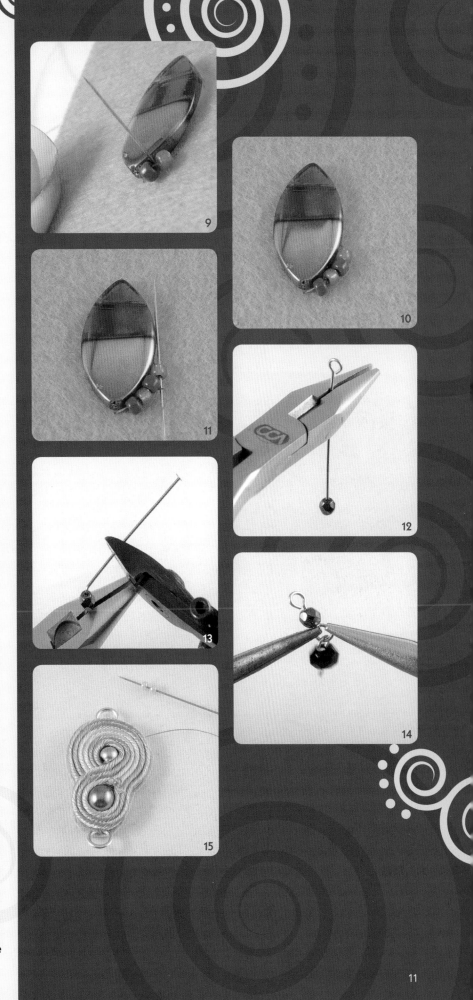

C. Sew down through the beading foundation just barely beyond the end of the fourth bead **(photo 10)**. Sew back up through the beading foundation so the thread is exiting just behind the fourth bead. Sew through the fourth bead **(photo 11)**, and pick up two more beads.

D. Continue the pattern of sewing up through the last bead added, picking up two beads, and sewing down through the beading foundation.

Bead chain

Bead chain is made of links, which are created by stringing a bead on a headpin and finishing each end with a **centered loop**. The links are then joined to form a chain.

A. String the desired bead or beads on a headpin and make a centered loop at the end **(photo 12)**.

B. Slide the bead(s) toward the loop. Use flatnose pliers to make a 90° bend just above the bead(s).

C. Use flush cutters to cut the headpin approximately ⅜" away from the bend **(photo 13)**. Use 6-in-1 looping, roundnose, or bail-making pliers to curve the end of the headpin into a centered loop.

D. Use two pairs of pliers to open one of the loops. Insert the open end of the loop through the closed loop of another link. Close the loop **(photo 14)**.

E. Repeat the previous steps until the chain reaches the desired length.

Brick stitch

There are a number of different edge beading techniques, some more decorative than others. Brick stitch is one of the most versatile, since the exposed holes of the edge beads allow you to join multiple components together.

A. Prepare the thread and **bury the knot**.

B. With the thread exiting the rib of the outermost layer of soutache, pick up two seed beads **(photo 15)**.

C. Sew through the rib of the soutache (approximately one bead's-width away from where the thread last exited), and sew diagonally out through the back of the

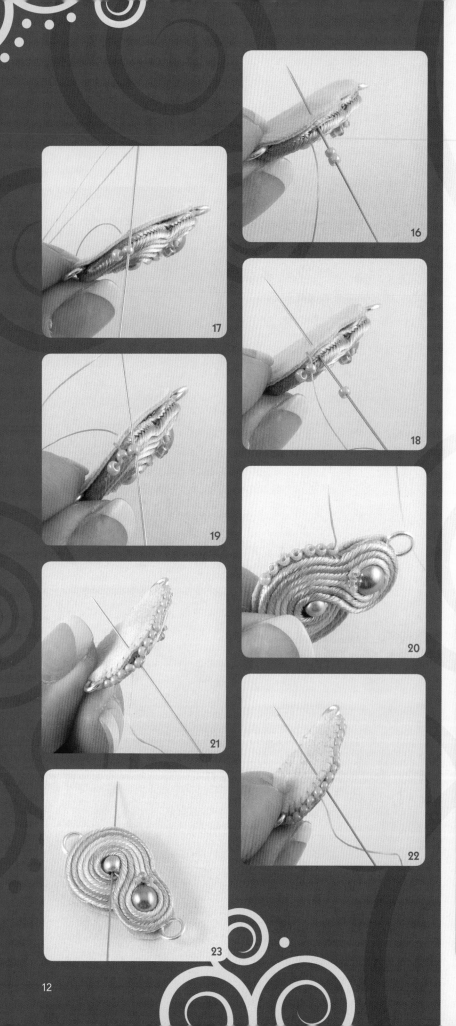

Ultrasuede very close to the edge (**photo 16**).

D. Sew up through the second bead so the needle exits between the last and the first bead (**photo 17**).

E. Pick up another bead, and sew down through the rib of soutache (about half a bead's width away from the edge of the last bead), and sew through the Ultrasuede very close to the edge (**photo 18**). Sew back up through the last bead (**photo 19**).

F. Repeat step E until you reach the first bead. After you've added five or six beads, you will begin to see that the beads "stand up" with their holes facing outward (**photo 20**).

G. Sew down through the first bead (**photo 21**), and sew through the soutache and the Ultrasuede. Sew back up through the first bead, and sew down through the second bead, soutache, and Ultrasuede (**photo 22**). **Bury the thread.**

Bury the knot

From the front of the work, sew through one of the larger beads and through the soutache (**photo 23**) so the thread is exiting the desired location. The knot will be buried inside the bead or between the bead and the inner braid of soutache.

MORE TECHNIQUES

Arabesque shape – p. 34
Asymmetrical split – p. 34
Buckle shape – p. 70
Concentric layers – p. 37
Curved ladder – p. 59
Eskimo slipper shape – p. 19
Halo shape – p. 49
Harp shape – p. 25
Koala face shape – p. 22
Ladder – p. 27
Layering components – p. 28
Lily shape – p. 30
Lollipop shape – p. 20
Open loops – p. 64
Negative space – p. 66
Rhinestone chain – p. 58
Parallelogram shape – p. 55
Soutache-wrapped strap – 82
Thread-wrapped strap – p. 74
Wrap a cabochon (with beads) – p. 45
Wrap a large bead (with soutache only) – p. 42

Bury the thread

Slide the needle underneath three or four of the **whip stitches** created by the edge beading (**photo 24**), and trim the thread. There is no need to knot the thread.

Centered loop

Use flatnose pliers to make a 90° bend approximately ⅜" away from the end of a headpin (**photo 25**). Use flatnose pliers to hold the base of the headpin. Use 6-in-1, rosary, roundnose, or bail-making pliers to curve the end of the headpin into a loop (**photo 26**).

Cover the crimp

Use flatnose pliers to close a crimp cover over a crimp bead or tube (**photo 27**).

Create a bridge

Bridges usually appear at **joins** and are decorative additions to the work.

A. Adjacent to any join, sew from the back of the work to the front so that the thread is exiting the innermost braid between the bead and the join (**photos 28**).

B. Pick up one small, one slightly larger bead, and another small bead. (This may mean an 11º, an 8º, and an 11º, or a 15º, an 11º, and a 15º, depending on the scale of the work.)

C. Stitch down through the front of the work at the corresponding point on the opposite side of the join (**photo 29**).

D. Sew back up through the work so the thread is exiting the innermost braid near and closer to the join. Sew through the middle bead (**photo 30**).

E. Stitch down through the front of the work at the corresponding point on the opposite side of the join. This second stitch secures the bridge to the work and creates a slight curve (**photo 31**).

ABOUT BRAID

The fine fibers of soutache braid give it two almost magical properties: First, it behaves almost like felt; stitches are easily anchored inside the fibers so, there is rarely a need to knot the thread before trimming it. Second, the fibers will open up or part, allowing stitches made carefully on the front of the work to sink into the braid and essentially disappear.

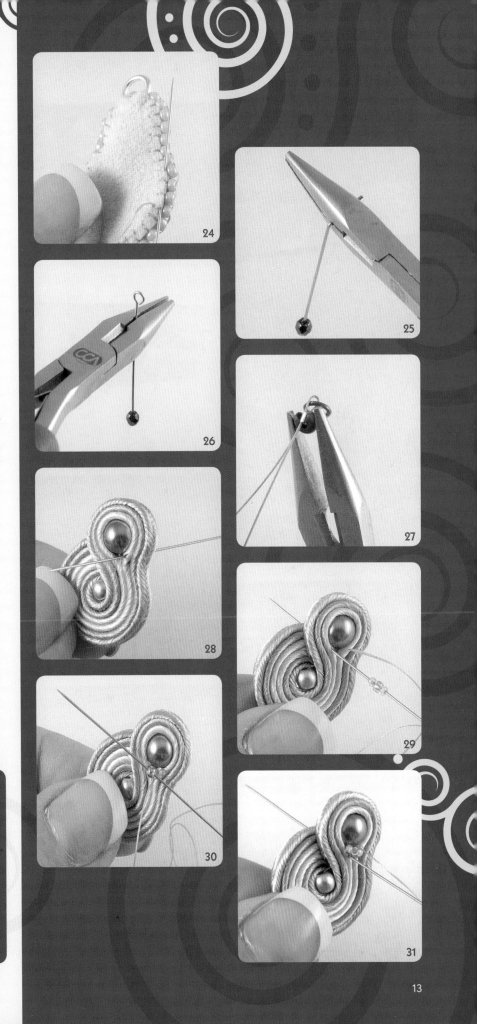

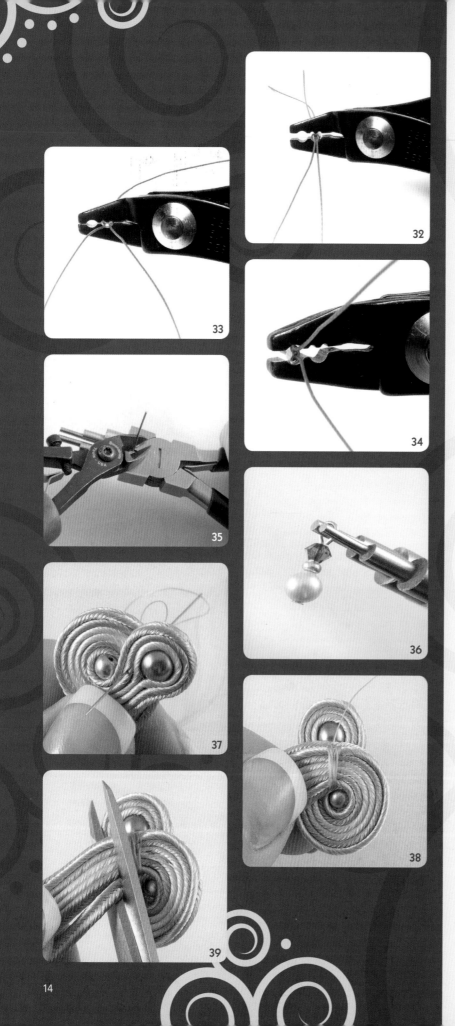

Crimping

A. Position the crimp bead in the hole of the crimping pliers that is closest to the handle. Holding the wires apart, squeeze the tool to compress the crimp bead, making sure one wire is on each side of the dent (**photo 32**).

B. Place the crimp bead in the front hole of the tool, and position it so the dent is facing outward. Squeeze the tool to fold the crimp in half (**photo 33**). Tug on the wires to make sure the crimp is secure.

C. Close a crimp cover over the crimp bead by gently squeezing with the pliers (**photo 34**).

Dangles

Slide bead(s) onto a headpin. Bend the top of the headpin 90°. Cut the headpin ⅜" from the bend (**photo 35**). Use looping pliers to bend the end of the headpin into a centered loop (**photo 36**).

Edge beading

(See **brick stitch**.)

End the stack

Holding the work between your thumb and forefinger, pull the stack behind the work. Secure with **tacking stitches (photo 37)**. Turn the work over and **whip stitch** through and over all of the braids in the stack (**photo 38**). Repeat three or four times (this will keep tail ends of the braid from fraying after they are trimmed). Trim the ends of the braid (**photo 39**).

End the thread

Staying on the back of the work, sew through a more layered area two or three times. Cut the thread (**photo 40**). There is no need to knot the thread.

Ladders

A ladder is any succession of beads stitched between two separated stacks; each stitch connecting the two stacks holds one bead. These connections become the "rungs" of the ladder. A ladder can be straight or curved, graduated or even, closed or open, connected or independent.

A. From the outside of the stacked pair, sew through the stack.

B. Pick up the desired bead. Sew through the second stack from the outside to the inside (**photo 41**).

C. Make one shaping stitch so the needle is exiting half a bead's width away from the edge of the last bead (**photo 42**). Sew through the stack.

D. Pick up the desired bead. Sew through the first stack from the inside to the outside.

E. Repeat steps A–D as needed (**photo 43**).

Prepare thread

Cut 36" of thread. Thread a needle, pulling approximately 9" through the eye of the needle. Tie an overhand knot on the other end of the thread (**photo 44**). Tie another knot directly on top of the first to double the size of the knot (**photo 45**). Trim the tail close to the knot.

TO BEAD OR NOT TO BEAD

As the craft of soutache and bead embroidery becomes more widely known, many talented artists are coming to the forefront, each with his or her own distinctive patterns and techniques. There are many ways of tackling soutache, and one question comes up quite often: Is edge beading really necessary?

The short answer is "no." There are many artists who simply glue on a backing. There are some who glue on the backing and whip-stitch around the edges. As a bead embroiderer from way back, edge beading was my natural go-to finishing technique—and after trying other techniques, I remain committed to edge beading. No glue is forever, and nothing makes me sadder than seeing beautiful work that is falling apart. An adhesive is a great placeholder, but stitching is the mechanical connection required to ensure longevity. Edge beading makes a beautiful finished edge that can easily be embellished, hides the outermost shaping stitches, protects the edges from wear and snags, allows components to be strung together, and secures jump rings deeply into the work. For me, the benefits of strength and durability far outweigh the expediency of other finishing methods.

I am a staunch, stubborn, steadfast member of Team "To Bead."

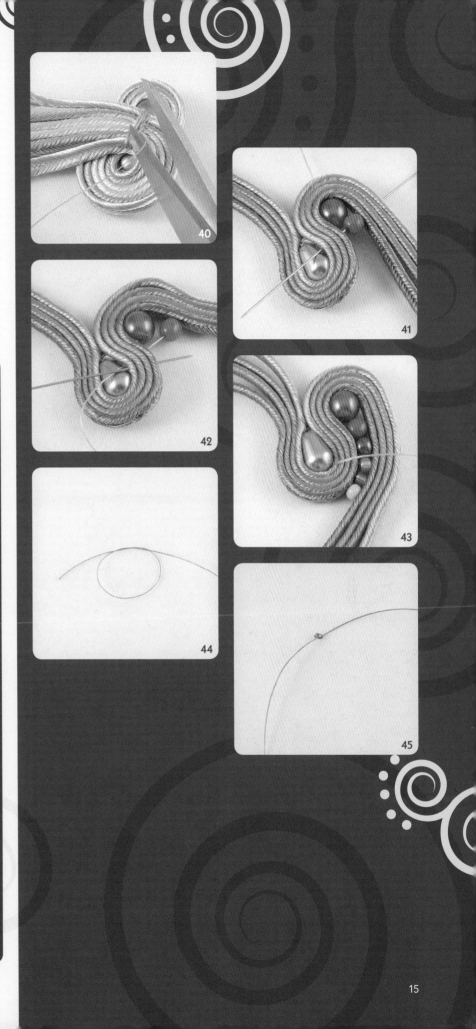

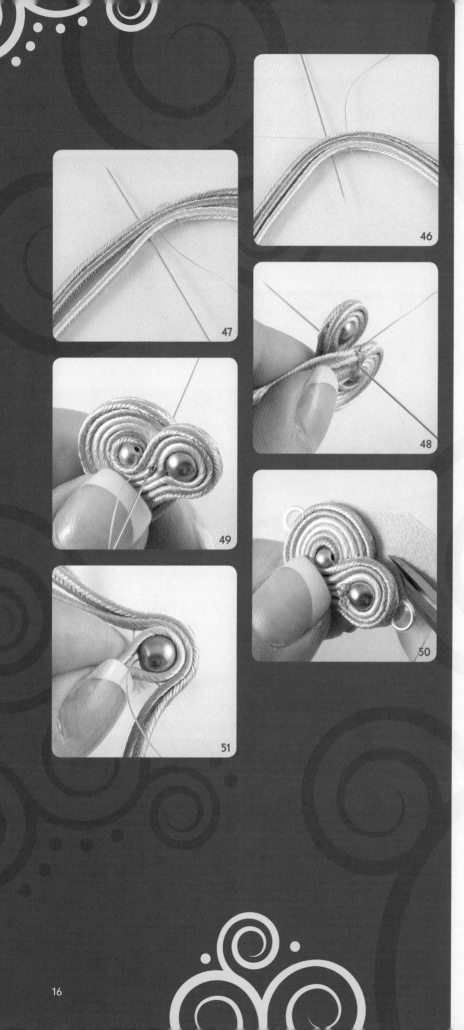

Shaping stitches

A variation on the running stitch, **shaping stitches** coax the soutache into the curve and hold it there. Shaping stitches should be longer on the outside of the curve—about ¼–⅜"—and shorter inside the curve (about 1⁄16"). Shaping stitches are always taken through the "ribs" of the soutache, meaning that the needle is driven up through the stack where the fibers of each braid come together in a v. The **stack** should be held in alignment so the needle passes through all the ribs in the stack. After completing several stitches, you will be able to feel when the soutache is correctly aligned because the needle slips through the ribs more easily than it will through the sides of the braids.

A. Holding the stack in the desired curve and working from right to left, sew down through the stack about ¼" to the left **(photo 46)**. (This counts as one **shaping stitch**.)

B. Sew up through the stack about 1⁄16" to the left **(photo 47)**. (This counts as the second shaping stitch.)

C. Repeat steps A and B as needed. A shaping stitch is one stitch, irrespective of length or whether it is inside or outside the curve.

Tacking stitches

Sew from the back of the work through the front of the work **(photo 48)**. Sew back down through all the layers as close as possible to the point where the thread exited **(photo 49)**. Repeat this step two more times, making each tacking stitch at a slightly different location.

Trace a path

Sometimes you'll need to get from one area of the work to another without pulling the work across the back or cutting and re-knotting the thread. Simply sew through the front of the work. Keep stitches inconspicuous by burying them in the soutache stacks and/or going through the holes of larger beads until the thread is exiting the desired location.

Training

While most of the process photos in this book are shown with the work lying flat on a surface, in truth, you will usually hold the work in both hands. Training refers to the practice of repeatedly stroking and curving the loose strands of soutache into the desired curve as you use **shaping stitches** to gently secure them into place.

Trim the backing

After glue has dried completely, trim the Ultrasuede. Be sure to trim the Ultrasuede from behind the exposed portions of jump rings **(photo 50)**. Do not over-trim; soutache should not be visible from the back of the work. It is OK if a thin outline of Ultrasuede is visible from the front of the work.

Two-sided join

A. Separate the stacks of braids where they meet, and pinch together the innermost braids of both stacks **(photo 51)**.
B. If the thread is exiting between the two innermost braids, sew through one braid only from the inside to the outside **(photo 52)**. (If the thread is exiting outside of the two innermost braids, sew through both innermost braids.)
C. Sew back through both innermost braids **(photo 53)**.
D. Sew back through both inner braids and the adjacent outer stack **(photo 54)**.
E. Sew back through the outer stack, the innermost braids, and the second outer stack **(photo 55)**. The braids have now become one large stack.
F. Keeping the thread close to the bead, retrace the thread path two or three times until the **join** looks clean **(photo 56)**.

Whip stitches

On the back of the work, sew through the ribs of the stack, pushing the needle away from you **(photo 57)**. Pull the thread toward you, and repeat **(photo 58)**. Repeat as necessary to bind the braids of the stack together.

CREATING BASIC SHAPES

Like most craft and art forms, soutache and bead embroidery uses some basic shapes over and over again. As you work through this chapter, you will master these shapes and learn to recognize them. Even the most elaborate necklaces or bracelets usually start with one of these core concepts, so it's helpful to be able to spot them in a piece.

The names (Eskimo slippers, koala faces, harps...) are simply what I call them. Over the years, as I worked on different projects, I often did collaborative work with my friend, Victoria Tane. I'd make little components that she would then incorporate into her fantastic, eclectic "Upcycled Jewelry." She'd call me and say, "Hey, can you make me a couple of those little three-bead puppies... the ones that look like little koala faces?"

And that's how it all began...

PRINCESS earrings

TOOLS

size 10 beading needle
scissors
flush cutters
flatnose pliers
looping pliers

MATERIALS

½ yd. ⅛" imported soutache in each of **3** colors
(mint, chartreuse, and mauve)

2 12x8mm teardrop beads (vitrail fire-polished)

2 6mm glass pearls (Czech, fuchsia)

2 4mm druk beads (Czech, silver)

2 4mm bicone crystals (Swarovski, palace
green opal)

11º seed beads

• 4g color A (transparent rainbow lime green)

• 1g color B (apricot ceylon)

4 15º seed beads (coral-lined crystal lustre)

4 6mm soldered jump rings (silver plate)

pair of ear wires (silver)

2 2" 21-gauge headpins (nickel)

Nymo thread, size B (rosy mauve)

2½x3" piece of Ultrasuede (glaze)

washable fabric glue

The first basic shape is the "lollipop," but the lollipop is not a finished shape—its stacks still need to be ended in some way to complete a component. The "Eskimo slipper" is the first possible finished shape you can make after having completed a lollipop. Work your way through the instructions for these delicate and sparkling earrings, and you'll learn how to make both the lollipop, which you will use as a nucleus for many other shapes and projects, and the Eskimo slipper, a wonderfully versatile shape that can be embellished in dozens of ways.

19

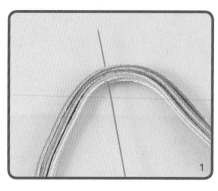

1

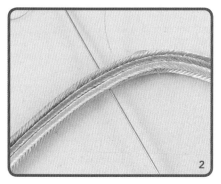

2

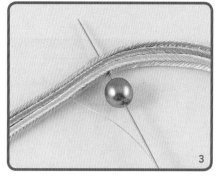

3

4

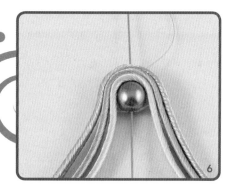

5

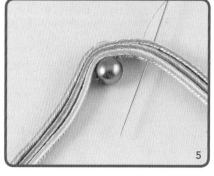

6

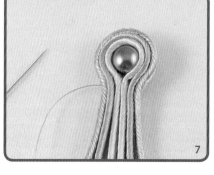

7

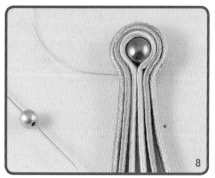

8

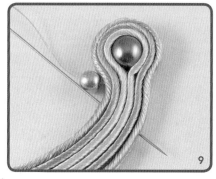

9

(Note that the Eskimo slipper is an asymmetrical shape. It may take a few tries to get a pair that are true mirrors.)

Start with a lollipop shape

A. Prepare the thread. Cut one 8" piece of soutache in each of three colors. **Align and stack** in this order: mint, chartreuse, and mauve. Locate the center of the stack, and sew through the stack from inside to outside, keeping the ribs aligned (**photo 1**). Working from right to left, make three **shaping stitches** (**photo 2**).

B. Pick up a 6mm bead, and sew up through the center of the stack near the knot (**photo 3**). Working from left to right, make three shaping stitches (**photos 4, 5**).

C. Sew through the 6mm and stack (**photo 6**). **Retrace the thread path**.

D. Make a **two-sided join** (**photo 7**). This shape (formed when a single bead is wrapped and the stacks come together in a two-sided join) is referred to as a "lollipop."

E. With the thread exiting the left side of the join, pick up a 4mm bead (**photo 8**). **Training** the large stack to the left, sew through the stack where the hole of the bead naturally meets the stack (**photo 9**).

F. Working from right to left and training the stack as you go, make three or four shaping stitches (**photos 10, 11**). **End the stack**.

G. Using a 15° seed bead, a color A 11° seed bead, and a 15°, **create a bridge** over the join (**photo 12**).

H. Add jump rings at the top and bottom edges of the work (**photo 13**).

I. Repeat steps A–H (training the stack to the right in step F) to make a mirror image of the first earring.

J. Apply backing to both components. Let dry completely. **Trim the backing** on both components, cutting the backing away from the exposed portions of the jump rings (**photos 14, 15**).

K. Use color B size 11º seed beads to **edge-bead** both components **(photo 16)**.

Assembly

A. String a teardrop bead and 4mm bicone on a headpin **(photo 17)**. Make a **centered loop** above the beads.

B. Connect the loop to a jump ring at the bottom of the component **(photo 18)**. Repeat to embellish a second earring.

C. Attach an ear wire to the jump ring at the top of the component.

D. Repeat steps A–C to assemble the second earring.

Delicate, airy soutache is perfect for creating substantial-but-lightweight earrings.

For some of the larger pieces in this book, you'll embellish with heavier stones, beads, and cabochons. But in this smaller, beginner piece, you'll find plenty of colorful style that won't wear you down!

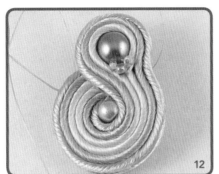

10

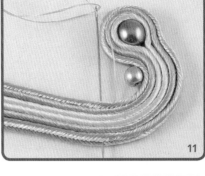

11

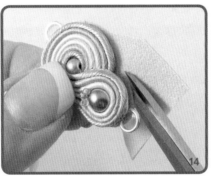

12

13

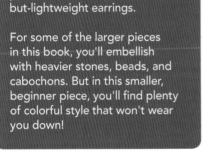

14

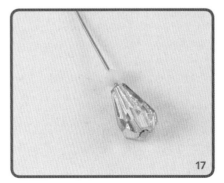

15

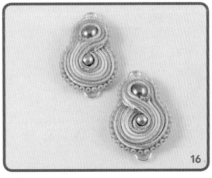

16

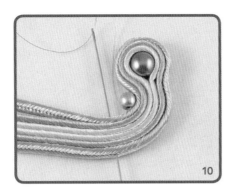

17

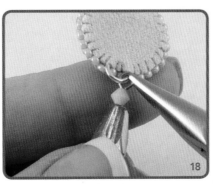

18

BASIC SHAPE: THE KOALA FACE
BONUS SKILL: STRUNG-BEAD CONNECTIONS

KOALAS ON PARADE
bracelet

TOOLS

size 10 beading needle

scissors

flush cutters

flatnose pliers

looping pliers

MATERIALS

1 yd. ⅛" imported soutache in each of three
colors (light yellow, reef gold, and dark taupe)

8 6mm druk beads (Czech, cream)

16 4mm glass pearls (cocoa)

10 4mm faceted round beads (Czech
fire-polished, gold)

26 8º seed beads

3g 11º seed beads (gold-lined antique white opal)

2 6mm soldered jump rings, brass oxide

2 2" 21-gauge headpins, brass oxide

6mm magnetic clasp (gold-plated)

Nymo thread, size B (gold yellow)

3x3" piece of Ultrasuede (gold medal)

washable fabric glue

The "koala face" is the second finished
shape you can make after completing a
lollipop. These symmetrical shapes can be
used alone, joined with other shapes, or
connected together to make something
as elaborate as a necklace. This bracelet
gives you the chance to practice making
consistent, symmetrical shapes. When you
have six even components, edge-bead
them, string them together, and—voila!—
koalas on parade!

Start with a lollipop

A. Prepare the thread. Cut one 6" piece of soutache in each of the three colors. **Align and stack** in this order: dark taupe, reef gold, and light yellow.

B. Locate the center of the stack. Sew up through the stack, keeping the ribs aligned. Use **shaping stitches** to make a lollipop around a 6mm bead (see p. 20) **(photo 1)**.

C. Separate the stack into two equal stacks. With the thread exiting to the right of the join, pick up a 4mm glass pearl. Sew through the stack where the hole of bead naturally meets the stack **(photo 2)**.

D. Working from left to right, make four shaping stitches **(photo 3)**. Pull the stack behind the work and **end the stack (photo 4)**.

E. Trace a path so the thread is exiting to the left side of the join **(photo 5)**. Use a 4mm and shaping stitches to make a mirror image on the left side of the join **(photo 6)**.

F. Use a 11º seed bead, an 8º seed bead, and an 11º to **create a bridge** at the join **(photo 7)**.

G. Repeat steps A–F five times to make a total of six components **(photo 8)**.

H. Add jump rings to two of the six components. On one component, the jump ring should sit between the "ears," and on the other, it should sit below the 6mm bead **(photo 9)**.

I. Apply backing to all six components. Allow to dry completely. **Trim the backing** from all six components. Be sure to cut the backing away from the exposed jump rings.

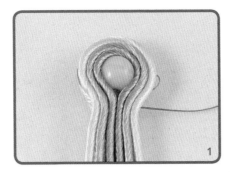

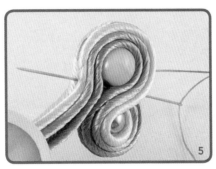

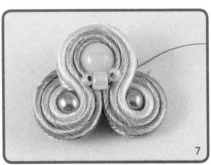

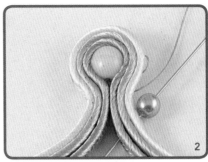

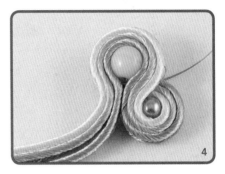

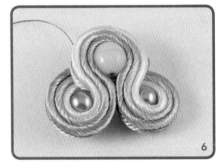

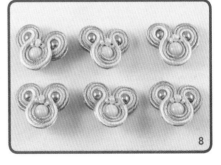

J. Edge-bead all six components using 11⁰s **(photo 10)**. Bury the thread.

K. Prepare the thread. Start connecting the components using **strung-bead connections; bury the knot** in one of the components that does not have a jump ring so the thread exits the edge beading at the top left as shown **(photo 11)**.

L. Pick up an 11⁰, an 8⁰, a 4mm faceted bead, an 8⁰, and an 11⁰. Sew through the edge beading of the component that has the jump ring attached below the 6mm bead at the top right as shown **(photo 12)**. Retrace the thread path twice so there are three passes of thread through the beads.

M. Trace a path through the front of the component so the thread is exiting the edge beading at the bottom right as shown **(photo 13)**. Pick up an 11⁰, an 8⁰, a 4mm faceted bead, an 8⁰, and an 11⁰. Sew through the first component at the bottom left as shown **(photo 14)**. Retrace the thread path twice.

N. Trace a path to the bottom right as shown **(photo 15)**. Continue making strung-bead connections between components, ending with another jump ring component. (You may find that for some connections, it's easier to make four passes of thread so you end up closer to your next exit point.)

O. String a 4mm pearl, a 6mm druk, and a 4mm pearl on a headpin. Make a **centered loop** at the end. Slide the beads to the loop, trim the head from the headpin, and make a second centered loop to create a link. Repeat to make a second link **(photo 16)**.

P. Attach a link to one half of the magnetic clasp. Repeat with the other link and other half of the clasp **(photo 17)**. (I find that it's easier to attach the links to the closed clasp and then pull the clasp apart.)

Q. Attach one half of the link-and-clasp assembly to a jump ring on one end of the bracelet **(photo 18)**. Repeat with the other half of the clasp and the other end of the bracelet.

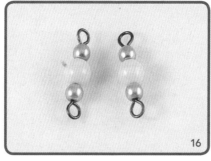

VIP
pin or pendant

TOOLS

size 10 beading needle

scissors

flush cutters

flatnose pliers

looping pliers

fine-point permanent marker

MATERIALS

1 yd. ⅛" imported soutache in each of three
 colors (dijon, rust, and willow)

2 9x6mm glass pearl teardrops (gold)

2 7x5mm glass pearl teardrops (gold)

6mm druk bead (Czech, gold antique)

2 6mm crystal bicones (Swarovski, olivine)

4mm druk beads
 • **2** color A (green iris)
 • **2** color B (matte gold)

4 6º seed beads (jonquil clear-lined papaya)

8º seed beads
 • **8** color C triangle (forest green-lined topaz)
 • **1** color D (olive metal matte)

1g 11º seed beads (sparkly green-lined pale
 amber round)

6mm soldered jump ring (brass oxide)

2" 21-gauge headpin (brass oxide)

1¼" pin back

vertical brooch converter

Nymo thread, size B (olive)

3x3" piece of Ultrasuede (fern)

washable fabric glue

The "harp" is the next naturally occurring symmetrical shape. Harps make great medium-sized earrings, and they can be used in groups or with embellishment to create much larger statement pieces. What sets harps apart from the shapes in previous projects is the addition of "ladders." A ladder is simply a row of beads stitched between two stacks. Ladders can be curved, straight, parallel, graduated, open, or closed. Getting your ladders smooth requires careful attention to thread tension. Bear this in mind as you're creating the outer curves of this piece: Use only enough tension to pull the stack into the desired curve. It is not important that the stack be pulled tight to the beads in the ladder. Once you see the curve you want, stop pulling!

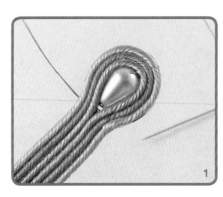

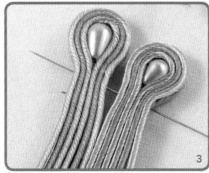

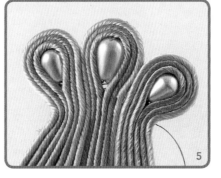

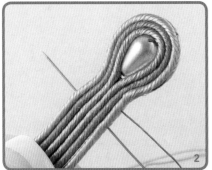

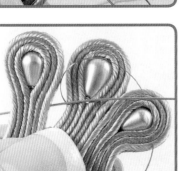

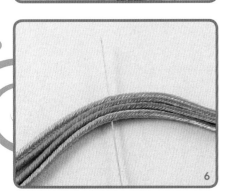

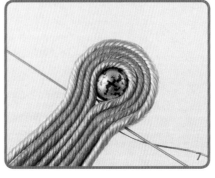

Component 1

A. Prepare the thread. Cut one 6" piece of soutache in each of three colors. **Align and stack** in this order: willow, rust, and dijon.

B. Locate the center of the stack. Sew up through the stack, keeping the ribs aligned. Use **shaping stitches** to make a lollipop around a 9x6mm teardrop bead (see p. 20) **(photo 1)**.

C. Use shaping stitches to secure the stack to about an inch below the join **(photo 2)**. Trim the thread.

D. Repeat steps A–C twice, substituting the 7x5mm teardrop, to complete a total of three lollipops, two smaller than the first.

E. Prepare the thread. Position one of the smaller lollipops to the right of the larger one. Sew through both large stacks beneath the joins **(photo 3)**.

F. Sew through the stacks again, about ½" further down the stack. Sew through the stack again so the thread is exiting to the left of the join on the larger lollipop. Position the second small lollipop to the left of the larger one. Sew through the join **(photo 4)**.

G. Sew back through the entire large stack. Retrace the thread path several times, adding tension until the lollipops begin to fan out slightly **(photo 5)**.

H. Use shaping stitches to secure the ends of the large stack about ½" below the joins. Retrace the thread path several times to secure the thread. Trim the thread.

I. Trim the loose ends of stack about ¾" below the joins. Set the component aside.

Component 2 (harp shape)

A. Prepare the thread. Cut four 12" pieces of soutache: one of dijon, two of rust, and one of willow. Align and stack in this order: willow, two rusts, and dijon. Locate the center of the stack. Sew up through the stack, keeping the ribs aligned **(photo 6)**.

B. Use shaping stitches to make a lollipop around a 6mm bead (see p. 20) **(photo 7)**.

C. Rotate the work so the 6mm is closest to you. Separate the large stack into two equal stacks, and **train**

the right stack into the desired curve (the thread should be exiting to the right of the join).

D. Pick up a 4mm color A bead, and sew through the stack where the hole of the bead naturally meets the stack **(photo 8)**.

Begin making a ladder

A. Working from left to right, make one large shaping stitch. Pick up a 6º seed bead, and sew through the stack, wrapping the center 6mm bead **(photo 9)**.

B. Working from left to right, make one small shaping stitch so the thread is exiting the stack approximately half the width of an 8º seed bead away from the 6º **(photo 10)**. Pick up a color C size 8º triangle seed bead, and sew through the outer stack **(photo 11)**.

C. Adjusting the length of the stitches for the size of the beads, work as in step B to add three more color C beads to the ladder **(photo 12)**.

D. Trace a path through the 6mm, and work so the thread is exiting to the left of the join. Working from right to left, make a mirror image on this side of the component **(photo 13)**.

E. Sew through the stack, wrapping the center 6mm **(photo 14)**. Pick up a 6mm crystal bicone, and sew through the left stack **(photo 15)**.

F. Retrace the thread path through the left stack, and sew through the right stack. Retrace the thread path through the right stack. Sew through the bicone and the stack wrapping the 6mm **(photo 16)**. Retrace the thread path through the stack and the bicone.

G. Make a **two-sided join** below the bicone **(photo 17)**.

H. Rotate the work so the 4mm beads are closest to you. Separate the large stack into two equal stacks, and train the right stack into the desired curve (the thread should be exiting to the right of the join).

I. Pick up a 4mm color B, and sew through the stack where the hole of bead naturally meets the stack **(photo 18)**. Working from left to right, make four shaping stitches.

J. Pull the stack behind the work. Use

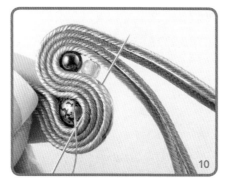

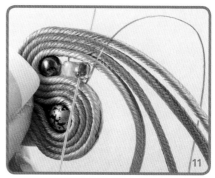

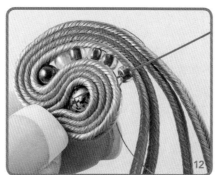

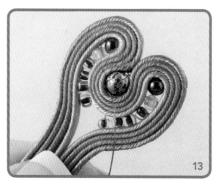

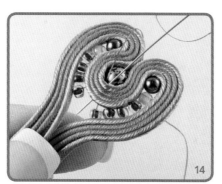

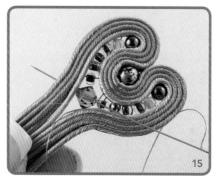

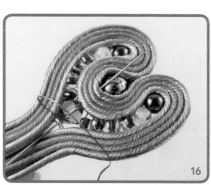

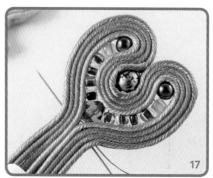

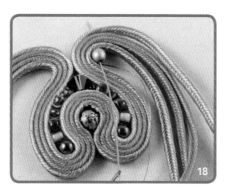

19

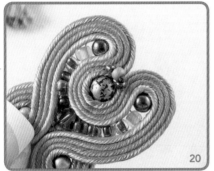

20

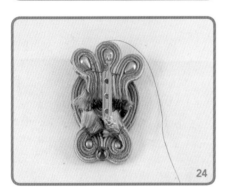

22

21

23

24

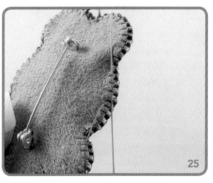

25

26

tacking stitches and **whip stitches** to end the stack.

K. Sew from the back of work so the thread is exiting to the left of the last join. Working from right to left, work as in steps I and J to create a mirror image **(photo 19)**.

L. Using an 11º seed bead, a color D 8º seed bead, and an 11º, **create a bridge** at the join over the 6mm **(photo 20)**.

M. Add a jump ring between the two color B beads **(photo 21)**.

Assembly

A. Position Component 1 behind Component 2 between the two A beads **(photo 22)**. Use tacking stitches to secure Component 1 to Component 2 **(photo 23)**.

B. On the back of the work, position the pin back so the hinge is closest to the teardrop end of the work. Stitch the pin back to the work, being careful not to sew it through to the front **(photo 24)**.

C. Fold a piece of Ultrasuede in half, wrong side out. Position the fold along the pin back, and use a fine-tip permanent marker to mark the locations of the hinge and clasp. Snip small openings at the marks. Be sure to snip vertically for the hinge and horizontally for the clasp. Test-fit the Ultrasuede over the work to be sure that openings slide all the way over the hinge and clasp.

D. Apply glue to the back of the work. Spread thinly. Avoid getting glue on the hinge or clasp.

E. Refit the Ultrasuede, wrong side down, over the pin back. Let dry completely. **Trim the backing.** Be sure to trim the Ultrasuede away from the exposed portion of jump rings.

F. Edge-bead the work using 11ºs **(photo 25)**.

G. String a 9x6mm teardrop bead, a 6º seed bead, a bicone crystal, and a 6º on the headpin. Make a **dangle**. Connect the dangle to the jump ring **(photo 26)**.

H. To wear the pin as a pendant, open a pin-back, slide the brooch converter over the pin, and close the pin back.

BASIC SHAPE: THE LILY
BONUS SKILL: PICOT EDGE BEADING

TRIPLE-SWIRL
necklace

TOOLS

size 10 beading needle
scissors
flush cutters
flatnose pliers
crimping pliers

MATERIALS

1yd. ⅛" imported soutache
  in each of four colors (pewter,
  copen, light turquoise, and orange)

3 9x6mm glass pearl teardrop (silver)

9 6mm druk bead (hot pink)

10 4mm druk beads (red)

8 6º seed beads (Czech, purple metallic)

8º seed beads
  • 2g color A (dove gray opal)
  • 2g color B (medium lilac opal)
  • 1g color C (dark yellow opaque)

3 6mm crystal bicone (Swarovski, Montana AB)

3g 11º seed beads (mint green)

1g 15º seed beads (Montana blue-lined
  crystal AB)

4 6mm soldered jump ring (silver)

2 2" 21-gauge headpin (silver)

4x4" Ultrasuede (silver pearl)

Nymo thread, size B (sterling)

2 ft. 49-strand beading wire

4 crimp tubes (silver)

4 crimp covers (silver)

toggle clasp

washable fabric glue

The "lily" is really just a harp taken a few steps further.
As you make this necklace, focus on symmetry; the
lily itself needs to be very balanced, and the Eskimo
slippers at the top of the piece should be almost
perfect mirrors of one another.

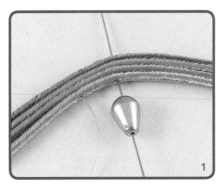

1

2

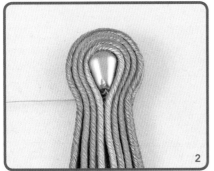

2

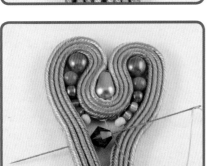

4

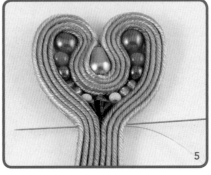

5

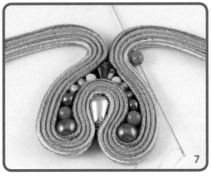

3

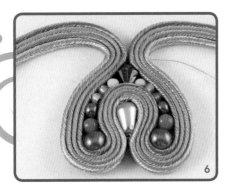

6

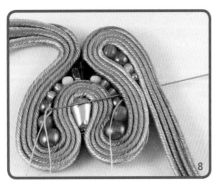

7

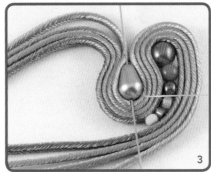

8

Center component, part 1 (lily)

A. Prepare the thread. Cut one 18" piece of soutache in each of four colors. **Align and stack** in this order: copen, light turquoise, orange, and pewter.

B. Locate the center of the stack. Sew up through the stack, keeping the ribs aligned. Use shaping stitches to make a lollipop around a 9x6mm teardrop bead (p. 20) **(photos 1, 2)**.

C. Using a 6mm bead, a 4mm bead, a 6° seed bead, a color A 8° seed bead, a color B 8° seed bead, and a color C 8° seed bead to make two ladders connected by a 6mm bicone crystal, continue working as in the harp (p. 26) until you complete the second join **(photos 3, 4, 5)**.

D. Rotate the work so the 6mms are closest to you. Separate the large stack into two equal stacks **(photo 6)**. The thread should now be exiting to the right of the join.

E. Pick up a 4mm and sew through the stack where the hole of bead naturally meets the stack **(photo 7)**. Using a 6°, an A, and an 11° seed bead, make a graduated ladder between the loose stack and the stack of the previously built ladder. Close the ladder by stitching the two stacks together **(photo 8)**.

F. Pick up a 4mm, and sew through the stack where the hole of bead naturally meets the stack. Make four **shaping stitches**, wrap the bead, bringing the stack behind the work **(photo 9)**, and **end the stack**.

G. Pull the thread across the back of the work and sew through the stack near the join so the thread is exiting to the left of the join **(photo 10)**. Work as in steps E–G to make a mirror image on the other side of the join **(photo 11)**.

H. Use an 11°, a C, and an 11° to **create a bridge** at the join under the teardrop **(photo 12)**. End the thread.

Center component, part 2

A. Cut eight 6" pieces of soutache, two in each of four colors. Align and stack in this order: pewter, orange, light turquoise, two copen, light turquoise, orange, pewter. Locate the center of the stack. Sew up through

the stack, keeping the ribs aligned.
B. Use shaping stitches to make a lollipop around a 6mm (p. 20) **(photos 13, 14)**. (Note: This is a larger stack, so you may need more shaping stitches to bring the stack smoothly around the center bead.)
C. Use an 11º, a C, and an 11º to create a bridge at the join under the 6mm. Trim the large stack **(photo 15)**.
D. Place Part 2 behind Part 1 as shown **(photo 16)**. Use **tacking stitches** to secure; end the thread.

Side components (Eskimo slippers)

A. Cut one 8" piece of soutache in each of four colors. Align and stack in this order: copen, light turquoise, orange, and pewter. Locate the center of the stack. Sew up through the stack, keeping the ribs aligned.
B. Use **shaping stitches** to make a lollipop around a 4mm (p. 20) **(photo 17)**.
C. Using a 6mm, continue as in the Eskimo slipper (p. 19) **(photo 18, p. 32)**. (Note: Because the stack is larger and the bead sizes are reversed, the resulting shape is rounder and fatter than previous Eskimo slippers. Adjust the length and/or number of shaping stitches to fit the larger overall shape.)
D. Use an 11º, a C, and an 11º to **create a bridge** at the join under the 4mm. **End the thread.**
E. Add a jump ring above the 4mm **(photo 19, p. 32)**.
F. Working as in steps A–E, make another Eskimo slipper a mirror image of the first.

Finishing components

A. Apply backing to all three components. Let dry completely. **Trim the backing** from the components, including the exposed jump rings.
B. Edge-bead all three components. If desired, add picot edge beading.
C. Bury the knot in the face of the work. Pick up two 11ºs, hold the work face down, and, working from left to right, sew on a diagonal through the rib of the soutache and the Ultrasuede two bead widths away from where the thread last exited **(photo 20, p. 32)**. Sew back through the second bead.

9

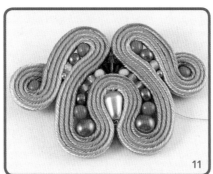

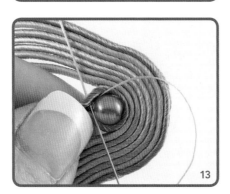

11

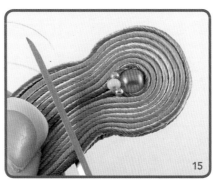

13

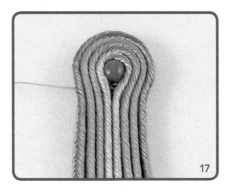

17

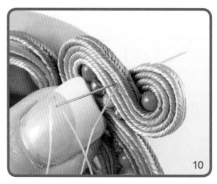

10

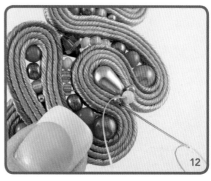

12

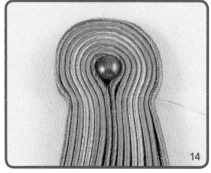

14

16

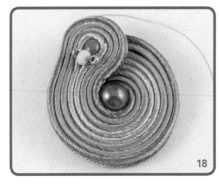

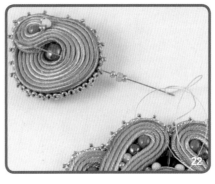

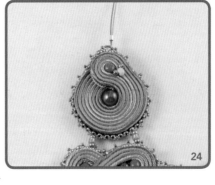

D. Pick up a 15º and an 11º. Sew on a diagonal through the rib of the soutache and the Ultrasuede one bead width away from where the thread last exited (**photo 21**). Sew back through the last 11º.

E. Pick up an 11º, and sew on a diagonal through the rib of the soutache and the Ultrasuede one bead width away from where the thread last exited. Sew back through the last bead.

F. Repeat steps D and E until the edge beading is complete. Notice that the 15ºs "stand up" on top of the 11ºs, forming a decorative picot. **Bury the thread**.

G. Use this picot edge beading technique on all three components.

Assembly

A. Bury the knot in the face of the center component so the thread is exiting the edge beading at the top left. Pick up an 11º, a B, and an 11º. Sew through the edge beading of the left side component as shown (**photo 22**). Retrace the thread path twice.

B. Trace a path through the side component so the thread is exiting the edge beading where shown. Pick up an 11º, a B, and an 11º, and sew through the edge beading of the center component (**photo 23**). Retrace the thread path twice. Bury the thread.

C. Work as in steps A and B to attach the right side component.

D. Cut 12" of beading wire. Loop the beading wire through the jump ring. String a crimp tube over both ends of the beading wire. **Crimp** the crimp tube (**photo 24**). **Close a crimp cover** over the crimp tube (**photo 25**). Repeat on the other side component.

E. String the remaining beads on the beading wire to the desired length. Use crimps to attach a jump ring to each end. Finish with crimp covers.

F. Use two 6mms and two headpins to make two **bead chain links**. Attach each link to a jump ring on one end of the strung beads. Repeat on the other side.

G. Attach the loop on the other side of the link to one half of a toggle clasp. Repeat on the other side.

ARABESQUE
earrings

TOOLS

size 10 beading needle

scissors

flush cutters

flatnose pliers

MATERIALS

1 yd. ⅛" imported soutache in each of two colors
(charcoal and pewter)

2 yd. ⅛" imported soutache (black)

1 yd. ⅛" domestic soutache (black-and-white
stripe)

2 10mm faceted glass round beads (smoke gray)

6mm beads

  • **2** color A (Czech, silver gray)

  • **2** color B (Czech, fire-polished, jet)

  • **2** color C (cat's eye, black)

4mm beads

  • **2** color D (Czech, fire-polished, hematite)

  • **2** color E (Czech, silver gray)

2 6º seed beads (black matte)

8º seed beads

  • **8** color F (jet matte)

  • **4** color G (gilt-lined, soft gray opal)

1g 11º seed beads (black diamond, silver-lined)

4 6mm soldered jump ring (silver-plated)

2 2" 21-gauge headpin (silver)

2 filigree bead caps (silver-plated)

pair of ear wires

Nymo thread, size B (black)

washable fabric glue

This will be the last basic shape that starts with the lollipop. It's not really even a shape—it's more of a concept. Up until now, every time you've made a join, you've then separated the large stack into two equal stacks. But what if you separated them into unequal stacks? The result is an asymmetrical shape that is reminiscent of arabesque design motifs.

If you don't have striped soutache, don't worry—just use what you've got on hand. But at some point, try working with some two-tone soutache. Its tiny pattern adds a whole new level of detail to the work.

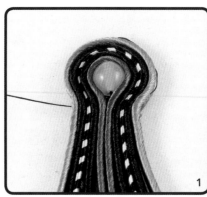

5

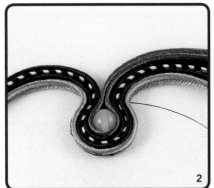

2

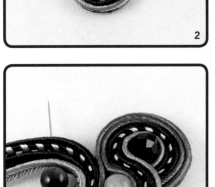

7

1

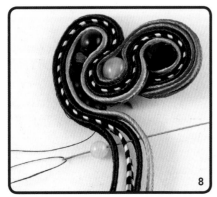

3

8

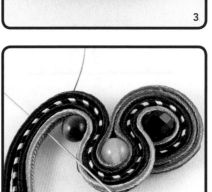

4

9

Start with a lollipop

A. Prepare the thread. Cut five 12" pieces of soutache: two of black and one each of pewter, charcoal, and black-and-white stripe. **Align and stack** in this order: charcoal, black, stripe, black, pewter (for best results, the stripe should be sandwiched between the solid soutache).

B. Locate the center of the stack. Sew up through the stack, keeping the ribs aligned. Use **shaping stitches** to make a lollipop around the 6mm color A bead (p. 20) **(photo 1)**.

C. Rotate the work so the A is closest to you. Separate the stack into two unequal stacks, with four braids curving to the left and six braids curving to the right **(photo 2)**. The thread should be exiting to the right of the join.

D. Pick up a 6mm color B bead, and sew through the stack where the hole of bead naturally meets the stack. Use shaping stitches to wrap the bead. **End the stack (photo 3).**

E. Pull the thread across the back of the work, and sew through the join so the thread is exiting to the left of the join. Pick up a 6mm color C bead, and sew through the stack where the hole of the bead naturally meets the stack **(photo 4)**.

F. Working from right to left, make one large **shaping stitch (photo 5)**. (Note: Think about where you want your needle to exit the stack. The next bead is going to be a 4mm bead, so where should the thread exit so the 4mm will fit comfortably next to the 6mm?)

G. Pick up a 4mm color D bead. Sew through the stack, wrapping the center A. Continue creating a ladder using one 6º seed bead and four color F 8º seed beads **(photos 6, 7)**. Retrace the thread path through the last F twice.

34

H. Pick up a 4mm color E bead, and sew through the stack where the hole of the bead naturally meets the stack **(photo 8)**. Make four shaping stitches, wrapping the stack around the E. End the stack **(photo 9)**.

I. Use a 11º seed bead, a color G 8º seed bead, and an 11º to **create a bridge** at the join over the center 6mm **(photo 10)**.

J. Add jump rings at the top and bottom joins **(photos 11, 12)**.

K. Make a second earring, reversing the apportionment of braids in step C so that four braids curve to the right and six braids curve to the left. Continue working to make a mirror image of the first piece.

Finishing

A. Apply backing (photo 13). Let dry completely, and **trim the backing**.

B. Edge-bead both components with 11ºs **(photo 14)**.

C. String a 10mm bead, a bead cap, and a G on a headpin. Create a **centered loop** above the G. Repeat to complete a total of two dangles **(photo 15)**.

D. Attach the loop of an ear wire to the top of one component. Attach the loop of a dangle to the bottom of the component. Repeat for the second earring.

9

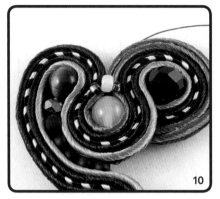

10

12

11

14

13

15

PINWHEEL *bracelet*

TOOLS

size 10 beading needle
scissors

MATERIALS

2 yd. ⅛" imported soutache in each of four
colors (chartreuse, delphinium, garden
rose, and rust)

6mm druk beads

- **4** color A (Czech, matte copper)
- **1** color B (antique gold)

4mm glass pearls

- **8** color C (olivine)
- **9** color D (burgundy)

10 8º seed beads (jonquil clear-lined
papaya)

12 10º hex-cut cylinder beads (metallic
rainbow gold/violet)

2g 11º seed beads (dark bronze)

.5g 15º seed beads (silver-lined smoky
topaz)

6mm magnetic clasp (gold plate)

Nymo thread, size B (gold yellow, light
purple, red, olive)

3 3x4" pieces of Ultrasuede (brass, fuchsia,
and fern)

washable fabric glue

I love beads—and I love soutache. Most often, I like my work to represent a balanced interplay between the two. But occasionally, I'll look down at a handful of soutache colors together and just fall completely in love with the material all over again. Concentric layers of soutache are a great way to let the braid have a little time to itself in the spotlight, and that's what this piece is all about.

This project is also an introduction to organic design. Rather than having a concrete pattern or final outcome in mind, begin creating from the heart, letting your eye tell you what to add. Once you've created a focal point, begin creating other small components to enhance it and complete the piece. If you are ever stymied by stitcher's block, gather the materials you love, and simply begin with no end-game in sight. The results will surprise you.

Circles

A. Prepare the thread. Cut a 10" piece of chartreuse soutache. Fold one end of the soutache length on a 90° angle 2" from the end.

B. Pinch the soutache just below the fold, and sew through the fold (**photo 1**). Pinch the fold a little tighter, and sew through the fold again in same direction as before.

C. Rotate the fold 180°. Sew through the fold and the newly wrapped layer of soutache (**photo 2**). Rotate the work 180°. Retrace the thread path through the work, including the newly wrapped layer of soutache (**photo 3**).

D. Continue rotating the work and sewing back through to wrap and connect layers until the work is about five or six layers across. Turn the fold 180°. Sew through the fold and the newly wrapped layer of soutache (**photo 4**).

E. Turn the work over so the short end of the soutache is sticking up (this is the back of the work). Sew through the outer layer on a diagonal, exiting the back of the work (**photo 5**).

F. Rotate the work 90° (this rotation wraps a bit more length of soutache around the core). Sew through the outer layer on a diagonal, exiting the back of work (**photo 6**).

G. Continue rotating the work and stitching on the diagonal, building up the diameter of the circle until you reach the desired size (mine is ¾"), exiting the back of the work (**photo 7**).

H. Pull the loose end over the back of the work. Use **tacking stitches** to secure the loose end to the back of the work. Repeat for the short end of soutache. Trim the ends.

Spirals

A. Prepare the thread. Cut a 10" piece of delphinium soutache. Sew through the soutache about 1½" from one end. Working from right to left, make one shaping stitch.

B. Pick up a color B 6mm bead. Sew through the braid approximately ⅜" to the right of where the thread last exited.

C. Pull the soutache around one side of the bead. Retrace the thread path through the braid, bead, and braid (**photo 8, p. 38**).

D. Wrap the long end of the braid over the short end. Sew through the braid, bead, and both layers of braid.

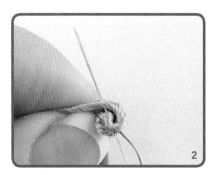
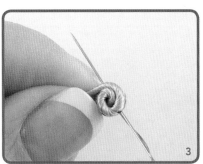
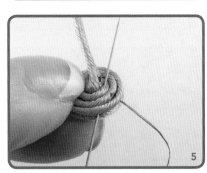
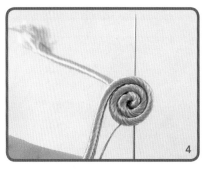
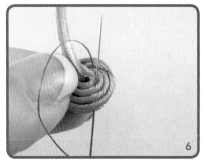
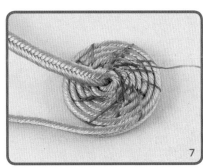

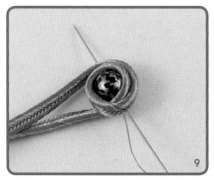

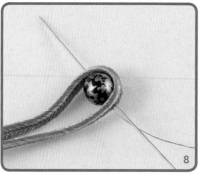

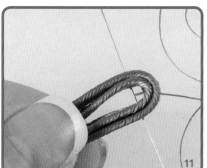

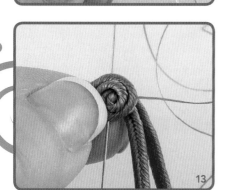

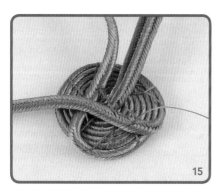

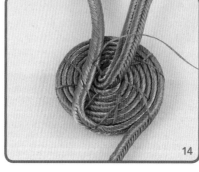

E. Rotate the work 180°, letting the longer end of the braid wrap the work. Retrace the thread path through the braid, bead, and braid **(photo 9)**. Rotate the work 180°, letting the longer end of the braid wrap the work. Retrace the thread path through the braid, bead, and braid.

F. Turn the work over so the short end of soutache is sticking up (on the back). Sew through the outer layer on a diagonal, exiting the back **(photo 10)**.

G. Rotate the work 90° (this wraps a bit more soutache around the core). Sew through the outer layer on a diagonal, exiting the back of the work.

H. Continue working and finish as in step H of "Circles."

Pinwheels

A. Prepare the thread. Cut two 10" pieces of soutache, one each of delphinium and rust. Align and stack in that order. Sew through the stack about 1½" from one end.

B. Fold the stack over the knot. Sew through both stacks close to the fold **(photo 11)**. Retrace the thread path.

C. Wrap the short end of the stack behind the long end. Sew through the fold **(photo 12)**.

D. Rotate the work 180°, letting the long end of the stack wrap over the fold. Sew through the stack and the fold **(photo 13)**. Rotate the work 180°, letting the long end of the stack wrap around the work. Sew through the work.

E. Continue working as in steps D–G of "Circles" until the circle is 2" in diameter. To end the stack, secure the inner braid first and then the outer braid **(photos 14, 15)**. Trim the ends.

Arrange the bracelet components

A. Make 10–15 circles, spirals, and pinwheels in multiple colors and sizes.

B. Measure loosely around your wrist, and add an inch. This is the finished length of your bracelet. Arrange the shapes in a pleasing composition **(photo 16)**.

C. Use **tacking stitches** to layer and connect shapes **(photo 17)** to create one large and two small components (I also left one circle, spiral, or pinwheel unconnected). Use **whip stitches** to attach a magnetic clasp half to the left end of the left small component and the other to the right end of the right small component.

D. Apply backing. Use a different color Ultrasuede on each component. Press the large component over a small cylinder (I used a candle jar) **(photo 18)**. Let dry completely, and trim.

E. Edge-bead all components using 11º seed beads.

Embellished edge beading

A. Bury the knot in the face of the work. The thread should exit the edge beading where you wish to embellish.

B. Pick up a 15º seed bead, a 10º hex bead, and a 15º. Push the beads down to the edge beads, and sew back through the hex bead.

C. Pick up a 15º, and sew down through the next edge bead **(photo 19)**. Sew up through the following edge bead.

D. Repeat steps B and C until the desired area is embellished.

E. On a new component, follow steps A–C, substituting 4mm glass pearls for the hex bead. Alternate pearl colors, if desired **(photo 20)**.

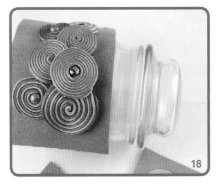

Assembly

A. Bury the knot in the face of the large component. Exit the edge beading at the top right, and pick up an 8º seed bead, a color A 6mm bead, and an 8º **(photo 21)**. Sew through the edge beading of the right-hand component at the desired location **(photo 22)**. Retrace the thread path twice.

B. Trace a path to the next desired connection point so the thread is exiting the edge beading. Pick up an 11º, a 4mm, and an 11º. Sew through the edge beading of the center component where desired **(photo 23)**. Retrace the thread path twice. Bury the thread.

C. Measure the work. Make another component, if needed.

D. Continue making connections as in steps A and B. Embellish other areas of edge beading as desired.

E. Make a swag (a longer connection) **(photo 24)**: Bury the knot in the face of the work so the thread is exiting the edge beading. Pick up a series of beads. Sew through the edge beading at the desired location, and retrace the thread path twice. Bury the thread.

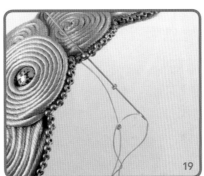

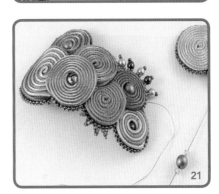

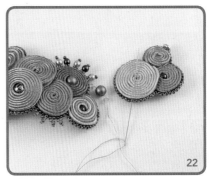

ADDING ELEMENTS

Once you've mastered the basic shapes, the natural question arises: "Cool. Now what?"

Well, there are many wonderful things in the beading world that are simply begging to take their turn with soutache and bead embroidery. Flat beads, cabochons, rhinestone chain—the list is long. The projects in this chapter are designed to dramatically expand your abilities. Because you've completed basic shapes in Chapter 1, you'll see that the instructions are written in a more simplified fashion; instead of 12 written steps designed to teach you how to create a lollipop, the instructions will now read simply, "Make a lollipop."

Don't worry – you can always go back if you need a refresher on something.

So go on…

Play with the new elements…

SUSPENDED STONE necklace

TOOLS

size 10 beading needle

scissors

flush cutters

flatnose pliers

looping pliers

permanent marker (purple)

MATERIALS

10" ⅛" imported soutache in each of five colors (purple, scarlet, antique, metallic bronze, and willow)

40x30mm flat top-drilled teardrop pendant (purple crazy lace agate)

25x18mm flat oval bead (purple crazy lace agate)

4 9x6mm glass pearl teardrops (bronze)

8x20mm treated quartz drop

4 6mm round beads (bronze)

8º seed beads
- **13** color A (olive metal matte)
- **8** color B (opaque frosted, red pepper)

1g 11º seed beads (topaz silver-lined)

2 6mm soldered jump ring (copper oxide)

4 2" 21-gauge headpin (copper oxide)

12" chain (antique copper)

toggle clasp (antique copper)

Nymo thread, size B (dark purple)

Fireline, size D (crystal)

1½x2" foundation

2x2½" Ultrasuede (scoundrel)

washable fabric glue

You now know how to wrap a small, round bead, but what if you want to wrap a *larger* bead? A larger bead will want to spin within the frame of soutache, which makes it difficult to get a nice, clean join. This project will explain how to overcome that obstacle.

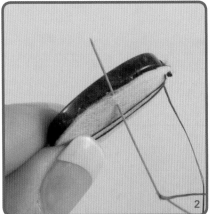

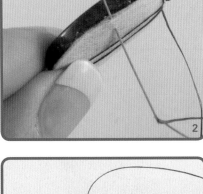

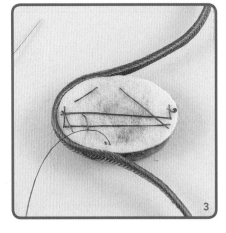

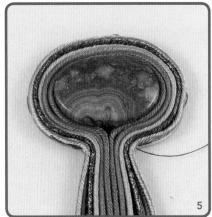

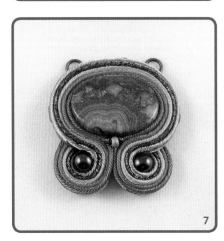

Center component

A. Color one side of the beading foundation with a permanent marker (don't worry about getting all the way to the edges or getting your color perfectly even—this is just to take the edge off the white).

B. Apply a small dab of glue to one side of the 25x18mm flat bead, and glue it to the center of the beading foundation. Let dry completely.

C. Cut five 10" pieces of soutache, one in each of all five colors.

D. Prepare the thread. Sew up through the beading foundation close to the hole of bead **(photo 1)**. Sew through the bead. Sew down through the beading foundation close to the hole of the bead. Retrace the thread path several times, keeping the thread close to the bead.

E. Trim around the bead. Be careful not to cut the threads. Keep a thin margin of beading foundation around the bead.

F. Working from the back, sew on a diagonal through the beading foundation so the thread is exiting the edge of the beading foundation at the center of one of the long sides of the bead **(photo 2)**. Sew through the center of the purple length of soutache at the rib.

G. Working from right to left, use **shaping stitches** to attach the single length of soutache to the edge of the beading foundation. Stop when you reach the point opposite the starting point **(photo 3)**.

H. Sew back up through the starting point. Working from left to right, attach soutache to the other side of the beading foundation. Sew back up through the starting point **(photo 4)**.

I. Align and stack the remaining four pieces of soutache in this order: scarlet, antique, metallic bronze, and willow. Locate the center of the stack. Sew through the center of the stack. Working first from right to left, use shaping stitches to attach the stack to the work.

J. Sew back up through the starting point. Attach a stack on the opposite side.

K. Make a **two-sided join** where the stacks meet **(photo 5)**.

L. Separate the large stack into two equal stacks. Pick up a 6mm bead, and sew through the stack on one side of the join where the hole of the bead naturally meets the stack. Wrap the bead, and **end the stack**. Repeat on the other side of the join with another 6mm **(photo 6)**.

M. Use an 11º seed bead, a color A 8º seed bead, and an 11º to **create a bridge** over the join. **Add jump rings** at the top left and right **(photo 7)**.

N. Apply backing, **trim backing**, and **edge-bead** with 11ºs. **Bury the thread**.

Add swags

A. Using a 30" piece of Fireline, bury the knot in front of the work so the thread is exiting the edge beading at the bottom left corner **(photo 8)**.

B. Pick up eight 11ºs, an A, a 40x30mm flat teardrop, an A, and eight 11ºs. Sew up through the edge beading at the corresponding right corner of the work **(photo 9)**. Retrace the thread path.

C. Trace a path so the thread is exiting the edge beading one bead to the left of the edge bead from step A. Pick up three 11ºs, an A, an 11º, a 9x6mm teardrop, an 11º, a B, an 11º, an A, a 6x20mm quartz drop, an A, an 11º, a B, an 11º, a 9x6mm teardrop, an 11º, an A, and three 11ºs. Sew through the edge beading one bead to the right of the edge bead from step B **(photo 10)**. Retrace the thread path, and bury the thread.

D. Make four **bead chain links** as shown **(photo 11)**.

E. Attach a loop on each of the longer links to a jump ring on the center component. Attach 6" of chain to the other end of each longer link **(photo 12)**. Attach short links to the other ends of the chains. Attach half of a toggle clasp to each remaining short link loop **(photo 13)**.

8

9

10

11

12

13

SHEBANGIN' SHIELD
necklace

TOOLS

size 10 beading needle

scissors

flush cutters

crimping pliers

flatnose pliers

looping pliers

MATERIALS

1 yd. ⅛" domestic soutache in each of three colors (merlot, ivy, and ruby glint)

polymer clay pieces

- 55x45mm shield-shaped cabochon
- **2** 45x35mm shield-shaped cabochons
- **4** 10mm lentil-shaped beads

5 14x14 mm puffed square beads (elephant skin jasper)

9 8x6mm fire-polished, faceted oval beads (Czech, bronze)

10 6mm druk beads (antique gold)

4 4mm druk beads (matte gold)

8º seed beads

- **50** color A (permanent-finish saffron)
- **90** color B (topaz, silver-lined)

11g 11º seed beads (matte gold)

2g 15º seed beads (transparent rainbow smoky topaz)

7 6mm soldered jump ring (brass oxide)

5 2" 21-gauge headpin (brass oxide)

4 #2 crimp tubes (gold-plated)

4 4mm crimp covers (brass oxide)

toggle clasp (brass oxide)

24" .018" 49-strand beading wire

2x4" piece of beading foundation (Nicole's Bead-backing, Beadwright, Orangey Orange)

3x5" piece of Ultrasuede (brass)

Nymo thread, size B (burgundy)

washable fabric glue

As if there weren't enough beautiful beads to choose from out there, life has to go and throw us cabochons, those delightful little flat-backed nuggets of loveliness that—alas and alack—have no hole. Not to worry! In this project, you'll learn how to create a peyote stitch bezel around a cabochon, which you can then treat just like any large, flat bead. For this piece, I used shield-shaped polymer clay cabochons made by artist Ann Dillon. Due to its light weight, polymer clay is a natural fit for working with soutache, and Ann's pieces, with their intricate patterning and organic textures, need little more than a soutache frame.

Creating peyote stitch bezels

A. Glue cabochons onto a piece of beading foundation. Let dry completely. Trim the beading foundation away from the cabochons, leaving a ⅛" margin of beading foundation around each cabochon (**photo 1**).

B. Row 1: Prepare the thread. Sew up through the beading foundation close to one of the cabochons. Using **backstitch**, surround the cabochon with a row of 11º seed beads (**photo 2**). (Note: You must have an even number of beads surrounding the cabochon. If you get to end of the row and there's only room for one more, leave a gap. It will disappear as the peyote stitch fills in.) Step up through the first bead in this row.

C. Row 2: Pick up an 11º. Skip the next bead in the previous row, and sew through the following bead (**photo 3**). Pick up an 11º, skip the next bead in the previous row, and sew through the following bead (**photo 4**). Repeat this stitch to complete the round. Step up through the first bead in this row.

D. Row 3: Pick up an 11º, and sew through the next bead in row 2 (**photo 5**). Repeat this stitch to complete the round (**photo 6**). Step up through the first bead added in this row.

E. Rows 4 and 5: Work as in step D to add two more rows, substituting 15º seed beads for 11ºs (**photos 6, 7**). Sew down between the peyote stitch bezel and the cabochon, and through the beading foundation. **End the thread.**

Up until now, every project has been made with imported soutache, which is a little thicker than domestic because it's more loosely braided. Domestic braid is thinner and more tightly braided, making it a better fit for use in smaller thicknesses that are less susceptible to snagging and fraying. I worked with BeadSmith to develop an extensive line of domestic ⅛" soutache. It is wonderfully consistent and its density allows for greater thread tension.

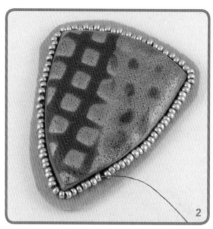

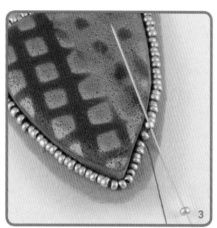

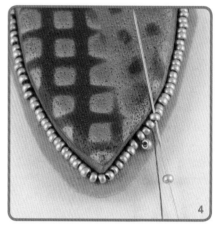

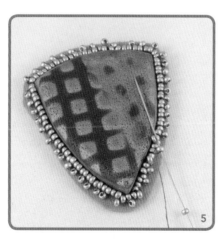

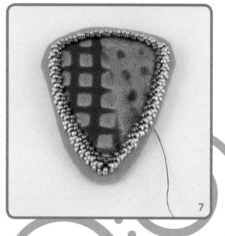

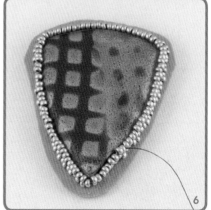

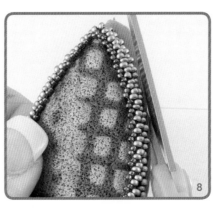

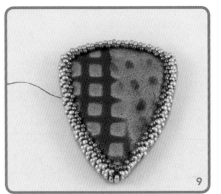

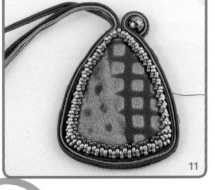

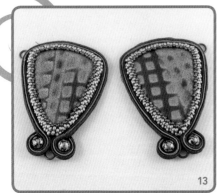

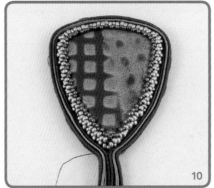

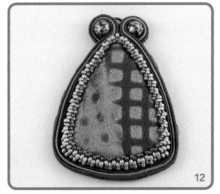

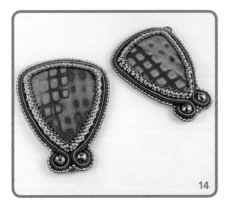

F. Trim the beading foundation close to the bezel. Be careful not to cut any threads (**photos 8, 9**).

G. Cut three 10" pieces of soutache, one in each of merlot, ivy, and ruby glint. Align and stack in that order. Apply the soutache to the edge of the beading foundation (see p. 42) (**photo 10**).

H. Rotate the work. With the thread exiting to the right of the join, pick up a 6mm druk bead, and sew through the stack where the hole of the bead naturally meets the stack. Use **shaping stitches** to wrap the bead. End the stack (**photo 11**).

I. Pull the thread across the back of work, and add a 6mm on the opposite side of the join. Use shaping stitches to wrap the bead. End the stack. **Add a jump ring** above the join (**photo 12**).

J. Repeat steps B–I to capture the other two cabochons. Add a jump ring to the outside upper corner of each of the smaller cabochon components (**photo 13**).

K. Apply backing and **edge-bead** (**photo 14**).

Assembly

A. Prepare the thread. Bury the knot: Sew through the bezel and soutache stack of the largest cabochon. The thread should be exiting the edge beading of the component at the upper left corner (**photo 15**).

B. Pick up a color A 8º seed bead. Sew through the edge beading of the left-hand cabochon at the upper right corner (**photos 16, 17**). Retrace the thread path twice.

C. Trace a path so the thread is exiting the edge beading of the left-hand component two beads away from the last connection. Pick up a 4mm bead and sew through the center component at the corresponding point (**photos 18, 19**). **Bury the thread.**

D. Work as in steps A–C to attach the right-hand component.

E. Cut a 24" piece of beading wire in half. Use crimps and crimping pliers to attach a 12" piece of beading wire to each of the two upper jump rings. Use flatnose pliers to press crimp covers over the crimps.

F. Use two headpins, two faceted oval beads, and four As to make two **bead chain links** as shown **(photo 20)**. Use three headpins, three oval beads, three puffed square beads, and nine As to make three **dangles** as shown **(photo 21)**.

G. String the remaining beads on beading wire in the desired pattern. End with jump rings, using crimps and crimp covers to secure the strung beads **(photo 22)**. Attach a faceted oval bead chain link to each of the jump rings. Add half of toggle clasp to each bead chain link **(photo 23)**.

I. Add each of the three puffed square dangles to the bottom of each cabochon component.

Metallic braid can add a lot of bling for your buck. Metallic soutache comes in two types: smooth and textured. I find the textured soutache much easier to work with; there are more open spaces for my needle to work its way through the braid, and the textured weave results in more twinkle. The trick to working with metallic braid is patience. The metallic fibers are usually a type of metallized plastic, which can easily snap, resulting in little cowlicks sticking up all over your work (not a good look). If your needle encounters resistance as you are sewing through the stack, fight the urge to just punch through. Rather, twist and wiggle your needle slowly. Your needle will find its way around the metallized fiber and out the other side.

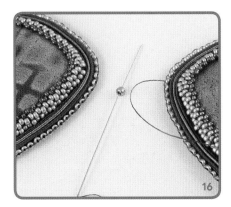
16

18

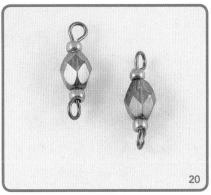
18

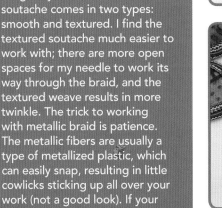
22

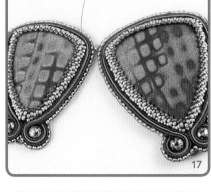
17

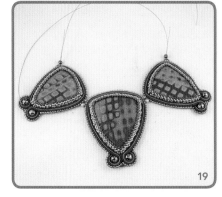
19

21

23

SPARROW'S NEST *earrings*

TOOLS

drafter's ellipse inking template

permanent marker pen

size 10 beading needle

scissors

flush cutters

flatnose pliers

looping pliers

MATERIALS

1 yd. ⅛" domestic soutache in each of five colors
(ivy, ivy-and-celery stripe, mint, textured
copper, and sage)

2 7x5mm fire-polished teardrop beads
(crystal gold)

6 freshwater potato pearls (**3** each of sand and
antique gold)

6 4mm glass pearls (olivine)

50 10º hex-cut cylinder beads (metallic rainbow
gold/violet)

1g 11º seed beads (metallic copper)

50 15º seed beads (silver-lined smoky topaz)

2 6mm soldered jump rings (oxidized copper)

2 2" 21-gauge headpins (brass oxide)

2 10mm flat-pad earring posts (stainless steel)

pair of earring nuts (yellow)

Nymo thread, size B (olive)

2x4" piece of Ultrasuede in each of two colors
(Fern and Topiary)

2x4" piece of Mistyfuse fabric bond

2x4" piece of Lacy's Stiff Stuff

washable fabric glue

Much of what I love about soutache and bead embroidery is wrapped up in the tactile qualities of the materials. The soutache itself, with its drape and sheen, is compelling to me. And, of course, I love the beads. But along the way, I developed an appreciation for other materials, including Ultrasuede. With its rainbow of saturated colors and soft, velvety texture, it does not always need to be relegated to the back of my work. Try this simple technique to make Ultrasuede a focal point in a piece.

A "halo" is a new stack connected to a secured stack by means of a ladder. This is one of the many ways to increase the size of your work, as well as add more color and texture.

Begin the component

A. Stack Mistyfuse on the wrong side of the fern Ultrasuede. Stack the beading foundation on the Mistyfuse. Following the manufacturer's instructions, bond the beading foundation to the Ultrasuede using a hot iron **(photo 1)**. (Be sure that no Mistyfuse is sticking out of the stack, since it will stick to the iron and burn).

B. Use the drafter's template, use a permanent marker to trace two ¾x1" ellipses onto the beading foundation side of your fabric stack **(photo 2)**. Carefully cut out the elliptical shapes, making sure the curves are smooth—any jagged edges will be seen on the front of the work. (You can reserve the remaining fabric stack for another project.)

C. Cut six 8" pieces of soutache: two of ivy and one each of ivy-and-celery stripe, mint, textured copper, and sage. Beginning with a piece of ivy, apply soutache to the edge of the beading foundation **(photos 3, 4)**.

D. Add the striped soutache and the second piece of ivy. Create a **two-sided join** under the ellipse **(photo 5)**.

E. Separate the stack into two equal stacks. Add and wrap 4mm glass pearls in each stack. **End the stacks (photo 6)**.

Add a halo

A. Working on the back, sew up through the edge of the beading foundation and stack at the center top. Pick up a hex bead. Align and stack the three remaining pieces of soutache in this order: mint, textured copper, and sage. Locate the center of the new stack, and sew through the stack **(photo 7)**.

B. Working from right to left, sew through the new stack one hex bead width away from where the thread last exited. Pick up a hex bead, and sew through the secured stack. Sew back up through the secured stack one bead width away from where the thread last exited **(photo 8)**.

C. Continue this halo pattern using hex beads, stopping one bead width from the 4mm. Work the last

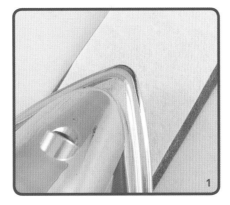

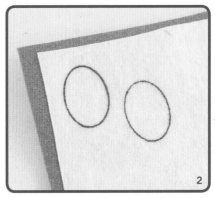

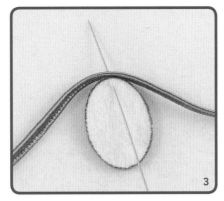

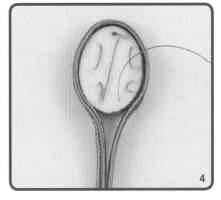

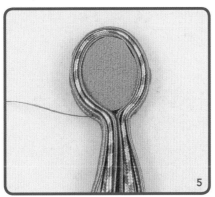

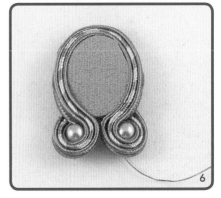

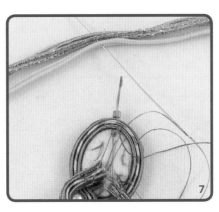

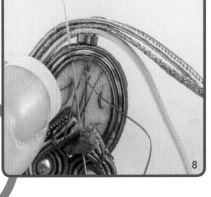

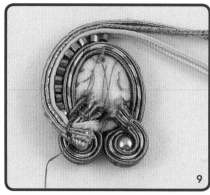

stitch with an 11º seed bead. End the stack behind the work **(photo 9)**.

D. Pull the thread across the back of the work and sew through the secured stack, hex bead, and new stack at the top center of the work. Working in the opposite direction, make a mirror image on the other side **(photo 10)**.

E. Using a 15º seed bead, an 11º, and a 15º, **create a bridge** over the join **(photo 11)**.

F. Sew up from the back of the work through the Ultrasuede just above the bridge. Pick up a freshwater pearl, and sew down through the work. Sew through the pearl again to secure.

G. Repeat step F twice to add two more pearls **(photo 12)**.

H. Sew up between the three pearls. Pick up seven 15ºs. Sew over the area where the two pearls are touching. Repeat this step twice as shown **(photo 13)**.

I. Embellish the areas around the pearls with 11ºs as desired. **Add a jump ring** under the join **(photo 14)**.

Assembly

A. Push an earring post through the wrong side of a 2x2" piece of Ultrasuede. Apply backing, and glue the work to the wrong side of the Ultrasuede. Make sure the disk of the earring post is completely covered by the work and is positioned near the top **(photo 15)**. Allow to dry completely, and trim the Ultrasuede.

B. Edge-bead using 11ºs.

C. Repeat to make a second earring.

D. Create two bead dangles as shown **(photo 16)**. Attach a dangle to a jump ring on each earring.

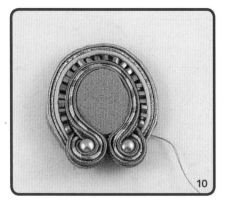

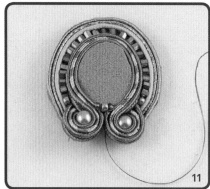

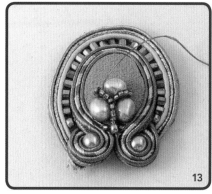

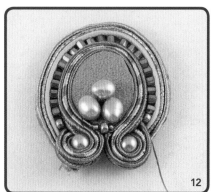

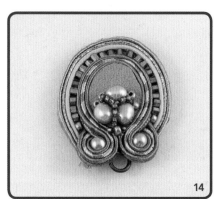

The lightweight nature of soutache jewelry makes it ideal for large, dramatic earrings. Learn how to apply a post finding (instead of a French hook), and you can max out the available soutache space between your earlobe and your shoulder!

BULLETPROOF
bracelet

TOOLS

size 10 beading needle
scissors
flatnose pliers

MATERIALS

1 yd. ⅛" domestic soutache in each of four colors
(blue, royal, navy, and gunmetal textured
metallic)

45x27mm cabochon (labradorite, irregular shape)

2 12x8mm polished teardrop glass beads
(purple iris fire)

6 3x10mm daggers (frosted light sapphire)

4 6mm fire-polished round (blue iris fire)

4 6mm glass pearls (Montana)

12 4mm druk beads (matte silver)

6 4mm fire-polished round (hematite)

2 4mm bicone crystals (Swarovski, Montana AB)

5 4mm glass pearls (Swarovski, dark purple)

9 3.4mm drop Japanese seed beads (matte
transparent capri blue AB)

4 #3 (¼") bugle beads (opaque powder blue)

8 6º seed beads (opaque cobalt)

8º seed beads
  • **34** color A (jet matte)
  • **40** color B (Montana silver-lined)

11º seed beads
  • **7g** color C (silver-lined gray matte)
  • **2g** color D (gunmetal)

60 15º seed beads (Montana blue-lined
crystal AB)

2"-wide dapped (domed) brass cuff

Nymo thread, size B (dark purple)

2 3x8" pieces of Ultrasuede (executive gray and
stone gray)

washable fabric glue

When I was a kid, I prayed every night that I would
be magically transformed into Wonder Woman. I
mean, really, the girl had it goin' on: the killer boots,
the invisible plane, and those rockin' bullet-deflecting
bracelets. And though I have long since stopped
wishing for a comic-book makeover, my fascination
with the big, chunky cuffs remains. I own lots, and
when I wear one (or four), I really do feel like I could
save the world.

Give your soft, silky soutache that bold geometric
form by applying it to a brass cuff blank.

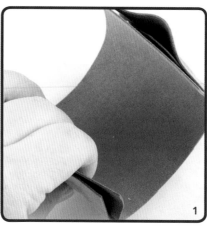

Prepare the cuff blank

A. Wash the cuff blank thoroughly with soap and warm water. Let dry. Open the blank as far as it will go.

B. Apply a quarter-sized dollop of glue to the outside of the blank. Spread a thin, even layer over the blank. Let dry for 1 minute.

C. Stretch the piece of executive gray Ultrasuede over the outside of the blank. Smooth the fabric with your fingers, and then let dry completely (don't worry if the Ultrasuede gaps a bit along the outside edges—this will get smoothed out later).

D. Apply a thin layer of glue to the inside of the blank. Let dry for 1 minute. Lay the stone gray piece of Ultrasuede into the cuff blank. Press and smooth the Ultrasuede onto the blank **(photo 1)**. Let dry completely.

E. Trim the Ultrasuede very close to the edge of the blank **(photo 2)**.

F. Prepare the thread. Sew up through the top layer of Ultrasuede near the edge of the blank. Pick up two color C 11º seed beads, and sew up through both layers of Ultrasuede approximately two bead widths from where the thread last exited **(photo 3)**. Sew through the last bead.

G. Pick up an 11º, sew through both layers of Ultrasuede **(photo 4)**, and then sew through the last bead again. Repeat this step all the way around the cuff **(photo 5)**. **Bury the thread.**

Center component

A. Glue the cabochon to the beading foundation. Let dry completely.

B. Using color C 11º and 15º seed beads, secure the cabochon to the beading foundation with a peyote stitch bezel as in the Shebangin' Shield Necklace (p. 45) **(photo 6)**. (Note: if your cabochon is tall, you may need more rows of 11ºs.)

C. Trim the beading foundation from the cabochon. Try to make your cutting line as smooth as possible.

D. Cut eight 10" pieces of soutache, two each of all four colors. Beginning with the blue soutache, apply it to one half of the edge of the beading foundation (p. 42). Apply the other piece of blue to the other half. The joins should be across from each

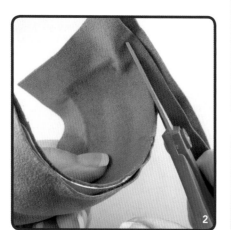

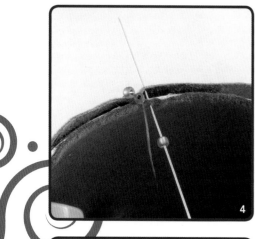

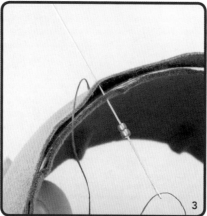

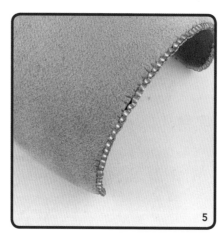

other diagonally (**photo 7**).

E. Align and stack three pieces of soutache in this order: royal, gunmetal textured metallic, and navy. Apply the stack to one side of the cabochon. Repeat with the remaining three pieces on the other side (**photo 8**).

F. Split the large stacks asymmetrically, with five braids to the left and three braids to the right. Add a 6mm pearl outside the larger stack, wrap it, and **end the stack**. Repeat on the other side with a small stack and a 4mm druk bead. Repeat with the braids on the opposite side of the cabochon (**photo 9**), making sure the large stacks are on opposite sides of the join.

G. Using a C, a color B 8° seed bead and a C, **create a bridge** at the join. Repeat at the other join (**photo 10**).

Side components

To make two arabesque shapes, follow the simplified instructions below or refer to p. 34 (**photo 11**).

A. Cut four 10" pieces of soutache in each of all four colors. Align and stack in this order: navy, royal, gunmetal, and blue.

B. Make a lollipop around a 12x8mm faceted teardrop.

C. Split the large stack asymmetrically, with five braids to the left and three braids to the right. On the left side of the join, add and wrap a 6mm fire-polished bead. End the stack. On the right side of the join, begin a graduated, curved, open ladder. Use the following beads in this order; a 6mm pearl, a 4mm fire-polished bead, a 4mm druk, a 6° seed bead, a color A 8° seed bead, and three Bs.

D. On the opposite side of the stack, add and wrap a 4mm pearl. End the stack.

E. Repeat steps A–D to make an identical (not a mirror) component.

Edge beading

Use Cs to **edge-bead** all three components without backing (**photo 12**).

Assembly

A. Apply glue to the back of the center component. Position the component on the center top of the

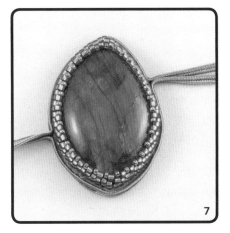
7

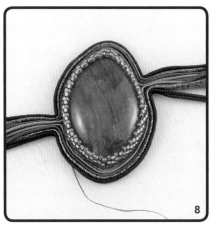
8

9

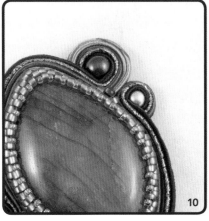
10

11

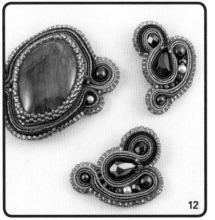
12

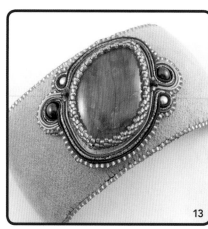

13

14

16

15

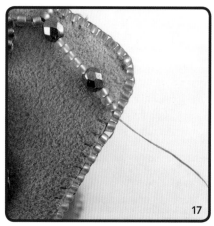

17

18

blank (**photo 13**). If the edges want to "lift," use clothespins to secure the component until the glue dries.
B. Apply side components in the same manner (**photo 14**). Let the components dry completely.

Branch stitching

A. Prepare the thread. Bury the knot by sewing through a 4mm bead near the edge of the center component. Sew through the stack and out through one of the edge beads.
B. Pick up four or five 11º seed beads. Test-fit the line of beads to see where they naturally meet the edge beading of the cuff blank. Sew through that edge bead (**photo 15**).
C. Sew through the adjacent edge bead. Sew down through the Ultrasuede and back up through the edge bead (stitching through the Ultrasuede secures the thread). Sew through the first edge bead and partway through the line of 11ºs (**photo 16**).
D. Pick up a line of beads. Begin incorporating some of the other beads in various shapes and sizes. Test-fit to the edge, and then sew through the edge beading of the prepared cuff (**photo 17**).
E. Repeat steps B–D, bringing branches of beads out to the edge of the cuff. (Slide your needle under the Ultrasuede just beyond the first large bead. This secures that longer line of beads tightly to the surface so it won't snag when worn. Do this as needed.)
F. Continue branch-stitching, making random angles and patterns. Keep returning to the center and side components, since branch stitching secures the components to the cuff.

Adjustments

Bend the cuff blank back into a curve to fit your wrist. Bending the cuff may expose the foundation. To cover the gap: **Prepare the thread. Bury the knot** in the face of the center component. Pick up four or five 11ºs, and sew through the beading foundation. **Trace a path** back to the last bead. Sew through the last bead, and add more beads as necessary (**photo 18**). Repeat on the other side.

BEAD-ME-DARKLY
necklace

TOOLS

size 10 beading needle
scissors
flush cutters
flatnose pliers
looping pliers

MATERIALS

1 yd. ⅛" domestic soutache in each of two colors (black and gunmetal textured metallic)

4 18x18mm rounded-triangular faceted beads (onyx)

5 8mm crown rosebud beads (hematite)

10 6mm Czech glass beads (silver gray)

3 12x8mm fire-polished teardrops (jet)

9 #3 (¼") bugle beads (hematite)

3 8º seed beads (gilt-lined soft gray opal)

2g 11º seed beads (hematite)

7" bead chain (silver/clear/gray beads)*

6 6mm soldered jump rings (gunmetal)

19 2" 21-gauge headpins (gunmetal)

toggle clasp (black finish)

Nymo thread, size B (black)

2x2" piece of Ultrasuede (black)

washable fabric glue

If you don't have pre-made bead chain, you can simply make your own by using more beads and headpins to make as many links as you like.

One of my favorite super-secret techniques is using bugle beads to make small "parallelograms." Depending on how they are joined to the work, these small forms not only add a contrasting geometric texture to the otherwise curvaceous world of soutache jewelry, but they can also evoke natural images such as leaves, flower buds, and birds' heads.

If you like your accessories a bit on the subtle side, use the soutache to make tiny individual components, and then treat each component like a bead. Pack visual interest into the smallest space possible.

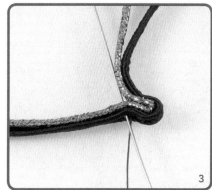

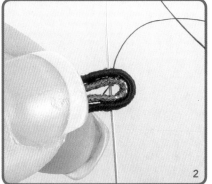

Make the component

A. Prepare the thread. Cut one 8" piece of soutache in each of both colors. **Align and stack** in this order: gumetal textured metallic and black. Locate the center of the stack, and sew up through the stack at the rib. Fold the stack in half over the knot **(photo 1)**. Sew up through both stacks, and sew back down through both stacks **(photo 2)**.

B. Repeat the stitch, adding a slight thread tension so the fold closes tightly.

C. Separate the large stack into two equal stacks. Sew up through the bottom stack only, very close to the fold **(photo 3)**. Pick up a bugle bead, and sew through the upper stack where the hole of the bead naturally meets the stack. Sew back down through the upper stack, the bugle, and the lower stack **(photo 4)**.

D. Working from right to left, sew up through the lower stack one bead width away from where the thread last exited. Pick up a bugle, and sew up through the upper stack **(photo 5)**. Sew down through the upper stack, the first bead, and the lower stack **(photo 6)**.

E. Working from right to left, sew up through the lower stack two bead widths away from where the thread last exited. Pick up a bugle, and sew through the upper stack. Sew down through the upper stack, the second bugle, and the lower stack.

F. Sew up through the lower stack, the third bugle, and the upper stack. Bring the lower stack up to the upper stack, and sew through both stacks **(photo 7)**. Retrace the thread path twice.

G. Working from right to left, make four **shaping stitches** through the large stack, curving the stack as you work **(photo 8)**.

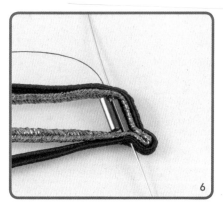

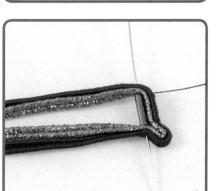

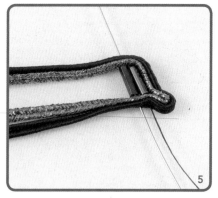

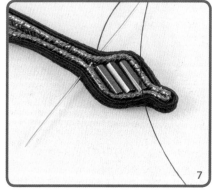

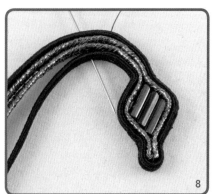

H. Pick up an 8mm bead, and sew through the join. Retrace the thread path through the join, the 8mm, and the stack. Working from right to left, make four shaping stitches, wrapping the 8mm **(photos 9, 10)**. **End the stack**.

I. Add jump rings, one at each end of the component **(photo 11)**.

J. Apply backing, and **trim backing**. Edge-bead using 11º seed beads **(photo 12)**.

K. Repeat steps A–J twice to make a total of three components.

Assembly

A. Use headpins and beads to make **bead chain links**: Make four links using rounded-triangular faceted beads. Make two links using 8mm beads. Make 10 links using 6mm beads **(photo 13)**.

B. Use headpins, teardrops, and 6ºs to make three **dangles (photo 14)**.

C. Connect components, links, and dangles as shown **(photo 15)**. Connect the bead chain to the last two links in the assembly. Add 6mm links to the end of the bead chain. Add a toggle half to each link **(photo 16)**.

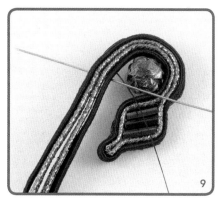

9

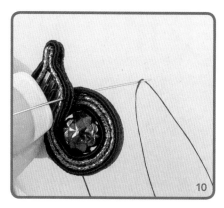

10

11

12

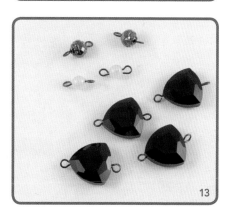

13

14

15

16

FULL-DRESS THISTLE
earrings

TOOLS

size 10 beading needle

scissors

flatnose pliers

MATERIALS

1 yd. ⅛" domestic soutache in each of five colors
(limelight, green, mint, lilac, and lavender)

2 10x14mm flat oval beads (dyed imperial jasper,
green)

2 8x12mm teardrop glass beads (vitrail
fire-polished)

4 2mm round beads (green, cat's eye)

4 6º seed beads (gilt-lined, olive gray opal)

8º seed beads

• **2** color A (jonquil color-lined papaya)

• **2** color B (dark green opaque luster)

11º seed beads

• 1g color C (sage green pearl)

• .5g color D (amethyst color-lined
magenta AB)

• **12** color E (silver-lined olivine color-lined
pink matte)

8 15º seed beads (Montana blue-lined crystal AB)

5" 2mm (14ss) rhinestone chain
(crystal/gold-plate)

2 6mm soldered jump rings (brass oxide)

pair of French hook ear wires

Nymo thread, size B (Sterling)

1x3" beading foundation (Beadwright, Nicole's
BeadBacking, chartreuse shine)

4x2" piece of Ultrasuede (fresh lime)

washable fabric glue

I use a lot of abstract shapes in my work, but I
love to make figurative pieces, too. Soutache, of
course, just cries out to be made into flower shapes.
Thistles are one of my garden favorites. They're
tenacious tenants, however, and are often viewed
more as a spiky weed than as a wonderful, structural
contrast to a sea of flowers. To emphasize my thistles'
significance, I've added some rhinestone chain. Learn
the trick to getting the chain to lie flat on your work,
and get ready to blingify an entire garden of blooms.

Frayed fringe is one of my favorite techniques. It
makes perfect thistle-fluff, but think of all the other
ways you could use it.

Center

A. Prepare the thread. Secure a flat oval bead to a 2x2" piece of beading foundation (see p. 42).

B. Cut a 2½" piece of rhinestone chain. Fit it around the oval **(photo 1)**. Position the chain so the end of the chain lines up with the narrow end of the oval. Sew up through the beading foundation near the oval, between it and the rhinestone chain **(photo 2)**.

C. Stitch over the connection between the first two rhinestones in the chain, sewing down through the foundation as close to the chain as possible. Sew back up between the oval and chain at the next connection, and continue stitching the chain down. (Don't stretch the chain; let the rhinestones sit fairly close together.)

D. Use flush cutters to clip off any excess rhinestones, and trim the foundation **(photo 3)**. Don't cut the threads, and keep your cutting line smooth.

E. Cut three 8" pieces of soutache, one each of limelight, green, and mint. **Align and stack** in that order. Apply the stack to the edge of the beading foundation (p. 42). Make a **two-sided join** at the center bottom of the work.

F. Divide the stack in half. On either side of the join, add and wrap a 2mm bead. **End the stacks (photo 4).**

Leaves and thistle down

A. Prepare the thread. Cut three 4" pieces of soutache, one each of limelight, green, and mint. Align and stack in that order. Locate the center of the stack, and sew up through the bottom.

B. Fold the stack over the knot, and sew up through the fold close to the knot. Retrace the thread path three times to tighten the fold **(photo 5)**.

C. Separate into two equal stacks. Sew up through the bottom stack. Pick up a color E 11º seed bead, and sew through the top stack **(photo 6)**.

D. Begin creating a ladder between the two stacks, but make each top stitch longer than the bottom stitch—work your needle on an angle relative to the line of the stacks. This makes the ladder curve slightly **(photo 7)**.

E. After the third bead, sew the two stacks together. Trim the ends close

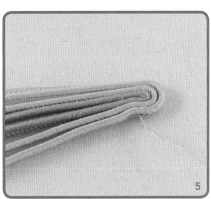

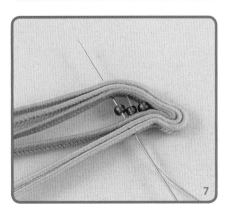

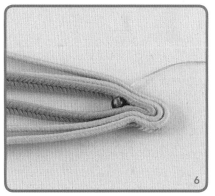

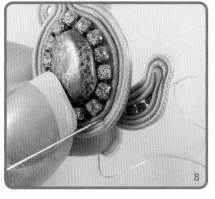

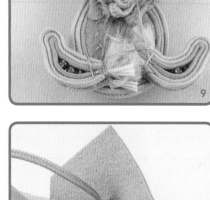

to the work. Place the leaf shape behind the center, and secure it using **tacking stitches (photo 8, p. 59)**.

F. Repeat steps A–E to make a mirror image on the other side.

G. Prepare the thread. Cut four 6" pieces of soutache, two each of lilac and lavender. Fold one piece almost in half so it forms a narrow v shape. Position it behind the center, and secure it in place using tacking stitches.

H. Repeat step G, alternating colors and fanning the pieces across the top of the work. Add a jump ring at the top of the work, positioned behind the join **(photo 9)**. End the thread.

I. Apply backing, and **trim the backing**. Be careful behind the top of the work—follow the outline of the center shape as if the vs were not there **(photos 10, 11)**.

Finishing

A. Prepare the thread. Bury the thread in the front of the work by sewing through the 2mm and the stack. The thread should be exiting just to the right of the vs.

B. Edge-bead using color C 11º seed beads **(photo 12)**. When you reach the v pieces, switch to color D 11º seed beads. When you reach the Cs, turn the work over and continue edge-beading with Ds across the top back.

C. Return to the front, and exit the first D. Pick up two Ds and a 15º. Sew back down through the Ds, making a tiny fringe **(photo 13)**. Make three more fringes across the top.

D. Trace a path to the bottom of the work so the thread exits the center bottom edge bead. Pick up a color A 8º seed bead, a color Bº 8º seed bead, two 6ºs, a teardrop bead, and a C. Sew back up through the teardrop, 6ºs, Bs, As, and edge bead **(photo 14)**. Bury the thread.

E. Lay the work on a flat surface. Press the point of a darning needle into the rib of one of the vs, and drag the needle toward the end to unravel the braid **(photo 15)**. Repeat several times for all the vs, moving farther up the braid as you go.

F. Trim the top of your thistle as desired **(photo 16)**. Add an ear wire, and repeat to make a second earring.

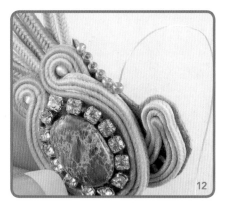

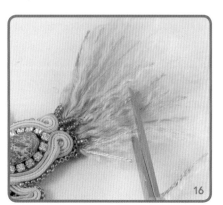

LAYERS AND LIGHT

Having mastered the basics, as well as incorporating various elements, one is inclined to go—well—a little nuts. Absolutely massive pieces of jewelry may seem to grow almost magically beneath your fingers, and chances are, you will fall in love with each and every one of them. As time goes on, however, you may notice a certain "heaviness" to the work. In spite of its actual light weight, soutache and bead embroidery can easily obtain significant visual mass.

This chapter introduces techniques that you can use to break up the volume of your work, adding depth-enhancing textures and allowing light to penetrate negative spaces and translucent elements.

Bead toward the light.

BEADED
lariat

MATERIALS

1½ yd. ⅛" domestic soutache, in each of four colors (royal, purple, cadet, and willow)

12x25mm marquise-shaped bead

12x17mm teardrop crystal (green AB)

4–8 6mm flat round wooden beads (navy)

4–8 6mm Czech glass round beads (frosted)

4–8 6mm Czech fire-polished beads

20–30 6mm bugle beads (green)

4–8 4mm glass pearls (lavender)

6–8 4mm bicone crystals (Swarovski, palace green opal)

6º seed beads
- **30–40** color E (blueberry)
- **30–40** color F (purple metallic)
- **30–40** color G (green luster)

8º seed beads
- **40–50** color C (gilt-lined grass green)
- **40–50** color D (414 opaque cobalt)

11º seed beads
- **6g** color A (durocoat mint green metallic)
- **6g** color B (cobalt clear-lined white)

.5g 15º seed beads (matte metallic patina iris)

30–40 "interest beads," such as cubes and barrels (these will be used for the cord parts of the lariat so, make sure they fit through the open loops)

2 crimp beads

2 crimp covers (brass oxide)

2 6mm soldered jump rings (brass oxide)

6 2" 21-gauge headpins (brass oxide)

Nymo thread, size B (royal blue)

2 yd. .018" 49-strand beading wire

5x4" piece of Ultrasuede (jazz blue)

2x2" piece of beading foundation (Nicole's BeadBacking, chartreuse shine)

washable fabric glue

TOOLS

size 10 beading needle

scissors

flush cutters

crimping pliers

flatnose pliers

By now, you've probably begun to realize how sensitive soutache can be; change the thread tension, and you change the shape. Change the height of a bead, and you change the shape. And while these nuances can cause you a lot of grief in the beginning, understanding how to manipulate this sensitivity opens up all kinds of new opportunities.

Component 1

A. Prepare the thread. Sew the marquise-shaped bead onto the beading foundation. The hole of my bead runs horizontally across the top, so I added a dab of glue to keep it from lifting up later on.

B. Sew up from the bottom of the beading foundation near the point of the bead. Using **backstitch**, alternate between colors C and D 8° seed beads to follow the curve of the marquise bead for one edge of the bead **(photo 1)**.

C. Sew up from the bottom of the beading foundation about half the width of a 6° seed bead away from the last 8°, and pick up a color F 6° seed bead and a color A 11° seed bead. Sew down through the 6° and the foundation. **Retrace the thread path** through the foundation, the 6°, the 11°, and back through the 6° and the foundation to stabilize the beads and keep them flat.

D. Using alternating colors E and F 6° seed beads, repeat step C, following the curve of the remaining side of the marquise **(photo 2)**.

E. Trim the beading foundation from around the work, being careful not to cut the stitches.

F. Cut four 18" pieces of soutache, one of each color. Beginning with the royal, attach the soutache to the beading foundation (p. 42) **(photo 3)**.

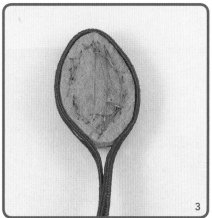

G. Align and stack the remaining three pieces of soutache in the following order: purple, cadet, and willow. Starting from the top of the marquise shape and stitching from the back of the work, use **shaping stitches** to secure the stack to the first piece of soutache and the edge of the beading foundation.

H. Make a **two-sided join (photo 4)**. Using an A, a bicone crystal, and an A, **create a bridge** over the join.

I. Begin stitching your first open loop: Straighten the soutache ends, and sew through the ribs of all eight pieces to create one large stack. Begin **training the stack** into a curve; use your fingers to shape the stack just slightly before each shaping stitch **(photo 5)**.

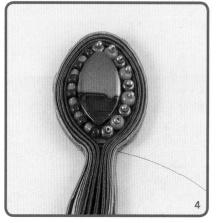

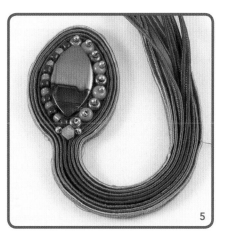

J. Keep making **shaping stitches**,

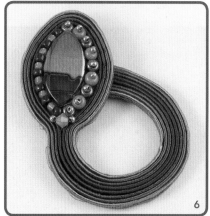

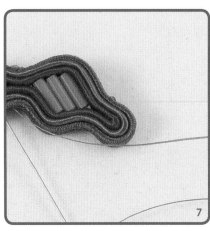

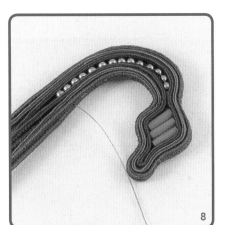

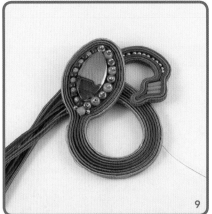

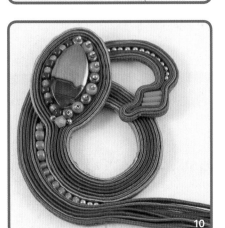

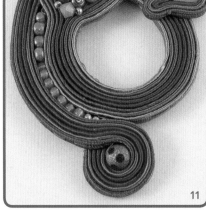

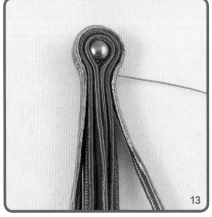

pulling the stack into the desired curve before each stitch, until the curved stack is the proper diameter to tuck behind the marquise **(photo 6, p. 63)**. **End the stack**.

K. Cut three 18" pieces of soutache, one of each color. Align and stack in this order: royal, cadet, and purple. Locate the center of the stack and, using three bugle beads, make a parallelogram (p. 55) **(photo 7)**.

L. Begin making an independent, curved ladder: Separate the stack, and sew down through the top stack. Pick up an A, and sew through the bottom stack. Sew back up through the bottom stack, pick up another A, and sew through the top stack.

M. Continue making a curved ladder. Each stitch across the top stack should be slightly longer than the stitch going across the bottom of the stack. This will pull the ladder into a curve. When the curved ladder has become long enough so that the last bead is about even with the beginning of the tip of the parallelogram **(photo 8)**, test-fit on the first component. The beading of the ladder should run behind the marquise shape, and the tip of the parallelogram should rest on the open loop **(photo 9)**.

N. If you are happy with the fit, use three or four shaping stitches to sew the two stacks of the ladder into one large stack. Fit the two components together again, and use **tacking stitches** to secure the second component behind the first.

O. On the back of the work, make a few more shaping stitches in the six-layer stack until the needle is exiting where the stack is extending beyond the marquise shape.

P. Working from the front and beginning just where the six-layer stack has begun to "appear" from behind the marquise, use four color G 6º seed beads, seven color C 8º seed beads, and thee color A 11º seed beads to make a closed, graduated ladder between the six-layer stack and the open loop **(photo 10)**. After the last A, connect the stack to the closed loop.

Q. Pick up a 6mm Czech round bead,

and sew through the stack where the stack naturally meets the hole of the bead. Use shaping stitches to continue wrapping the bead. **End the stack**, and then end the thread **(photo 11)**.

R. Prepare the thread. Use **tacking stitches** to secure the parallelogram to the open loop where the two meet **(photo 12)**.

Component 2

A. Cut three 18" pieces of soutache, one of each color (cadet, purple, and willow). Align and stack. Locate the center of the stack, and use a 4mm glass pearl to make a lollipop **(photo 13)**.

B. Use three bugle beads to create a parallelogram **(photo 14)**.

C. Separate the large stack into two equal stacks. With the thread exiting left of the join, pick up a 6mm fire-polished bead, and sew through the left stack where the hole of the bead naturally meets the stack. Use shaping stitches to wrap the bead, and end the stack.

D. With the thread exiting the soutache to the right of the join, pick up a 6mm wooden bead, and sew through the first two pieces of soutache in the stack only where the hole of the bead naturally meets the stack **(photo 15)**. Wrap the bead, and end the stack. Trace a path so the thread is exiting the outer layer of soutache, wrapping the wooden bead near the join.

E. Cut a 6" piece of royal soutache. Sew through the third piece of soutache (the loose one) in the right-hand stack and the new 6" piece about 2" from the end **(photo 16)**. Beginning with a color A 11º seed bead and continuing with alternating colors C and D 8º seed beads, create a curved ladder between the loose stack and the stack wrapping the wooden bead **(photo 17)**. **End the stack**.

Finishing the components

A. Apply the backing, let dry completely, and **trim (photo 18)**. (Don't trim the backing from the negative spaces yet.)

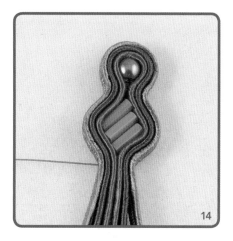

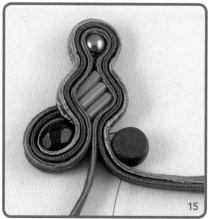

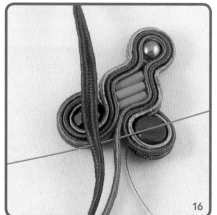

21

22

23

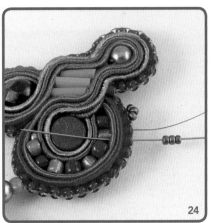

24

25

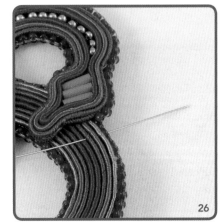

26

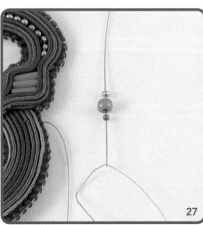

27

B. Edge-bead both components using color B 11º seed beads **(photo 19, p. 65)**. **Bury the thread**.
C. Use a darning needle to gently make a hole in the middle of one of the negative spaces. Using the small hole as a starting point, carefully trim away the backing from the negative space with small scissors **(photo 20, p. 65)**. Don't trim away too much and expose the soutache from the back. Repeat for the second negative space.
D. Edge-bead the negative spaces using Bs. **Bury the thread**.

Connecting components

A. Prepare the thread. Bury the knot in Component 2, and sew through the edge-beading so the thread is exiting at the bottom of the wooden bead.
B. Pick up a color C 8º seed bead, a 4mm glass pearl, and a C, and sew through Component 1 where indicated **(photo 21)**. Retrace the thread path twice.
C. Trace a path so the thread is exiting Component 1. Pick up a color A 11º seed bead, a color D 8º seed bead, a color F 6º seed bead, a 6mm Czech round frosted bead, an F, a D, and an A, and sew through the edge beading of Component 2 **(photo 22)**. Retrace the thread path twice. Bury the thread.

Embellished edge beading (optional)

A. Prepare the thread. Bury the knot in Component 2 so the thread is exiting the edge beading as shown **(photo 23)**. Pick up three 15º seed beads, and sew through the edge bead and the stack to the right of the first **(photo 24)**.
B. Sew through the stack and the edge bead to the right of the last.
C. Pick up three 15ºs, and sew down through the next edge bead and stack. Repeat as desired **(photo 25)**. Bury the thread.
D. Prepare the thread. Bury the knot in Component 1 so the thread is exiting the edge beading where indicated **(photo 26)**. Pick up a 15º, a color E 6º seed bead, and an A. Sew

back through the E and pick up a 15º **(photos 27, 28)**.

E. Sew through the edge bead and the stack to the right of the first, and then sew through the stack and edge bead to the right of the last **(photo 29)**.

F. Repeat steps D and E as many times as desired, alternating the color of the 6º. Bury the thread.

Add cords

A. Poke one end of 2-yd. piece of beading wire through the edge beading at the top of Component 2. Poke the other end of the beading wire through the adjacent edge bead **(photo 30)**.

B. On one of the two strands, begin stringing the remaining beads in a semi-random pattern **(photo 31)** (I used 10–15 11º seed beads, a couple of larger interest beads, 10–15 more 11ºs, and so on). When you have about 3" of beading wire left, string a crimp tube and a jump ring.

C. Thread the beading wire back through the crimp tube and the last three or four strung beads. Pull the beading wire snug. Use crimping pliers to crimp the crimp tube, and press a crimp cover over the crimp **(photo 32)**. Trim any excess beading wire.

D. Repeat steps B and C for the second strand.

Make dangles

A. Use seed beads and interest beads to make six dangles of varying lengths **(photo 33)**. Hang three dangles from each of the two jump rings.

B. To wear the necklace, thread both cords through the front of the work.

28

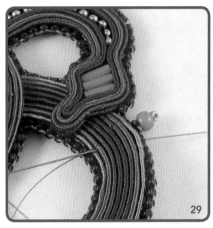
29

30

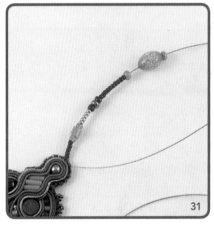
31

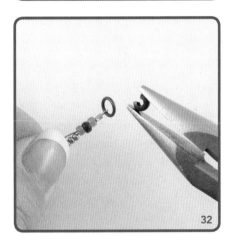
32

33

NOUVEAU BLUES *earrings*

TOOLS

size 10 beading needle

scissors

flatnose pliers

MATERIALS

2 yd. ⅛" domestic soutache in each of four colors (peacock, duck, medium blue, and rainbow metallic)

2 17x8mm spindle beads (opaque aqua)

10 6mm druk beads (ivory)

4 6º seed beads (gilt-lined antique white opal)

8º seed beads
- **32** color A (hex, light jonquil-lined aqua)
- **16** color B (gilt-lined antique white opal)

11º seed beads
- **4** color C (permanent galvanized silver matte)
- 2g color D (color-lined capri)

6 5x5mm bead caps (silver finish)

2 6mm soldered jump rings (silver finish)

2 French hook ear wires (silver)

4x4" piece of Ultrasuede (jazz blue)

2x2" piece of beading foundation (optional)

Nymo thread, size B (turquoise)

washable fabric glue

There are many different ways to add layers to your work to increase the level of interest and complexity. The simplest, layering components, was explored in the "VIP Pin or Pendant" (p. 28), when you attached the second part of a center component behind the first. Halos (ladders that are created between an existing, secured stack and a new, entirely separate stack, forming a new curve of beads and soutache) were incorporated in the "Sparrow's Nest Earrings" (p. 49). "Buckles" are curved ladders made completely separate from the existing work and then wrapped over a portion of the design. You will use all three techniques in these elegantly elaborate earrings.

Bead caps—wondrous little findings that fit over the top of a bead—can enhance your work beautifully. First, if you have mostly round beads, bead caps basically double the number of shapes available to you. After all, what is a teardrop shape but a sphere with a cone on one end? Furthermore, the addition of the caps allows you to quickly and easily incorporate yet another element or texture into your work, adding to the visual richness of your finished piece.

Part 1

A. Prepare the thread. Cut one 8" piece of soutache in each color. **Align and stack** in this order: peacock, rainbow metallic, medium blue, and duck.

B. Make a lollipop around a spindle bead **(photo 1)**. I made my lollipop without any beading foundation, but these beads are large. You can use the technique taught in the "Suspended Stone Necklace" (see p. 42).

(see p. 42)

C. Use **shaping stitches** to secure the large stack together to a length of about ¾" beyond the join **(photo 2)**.

D. Trace a path so the thread is exiting the stack, wrapping the spindle on the end opposite the join. Pick up an 8º hex bead.

E. Cut two 8" pieces of medium blue soutache. **Align and stack.** Locate the center of the stack, and sew through the center. Working from right to left and using hex beads, begin making a halo (see p. 49) around the work until you have a total of eight hex beads incorporated **(photo 3)**. Add a color C size 11º seed bead to the halo.

(see p. 49)

F. Sew the working stack to the secured stack **(photo 4)**. **Retrace the thread path.**

G. Pick up a 6mm bead. Sew through the stack where the hole of the bead naturally meets the stack. Wrap the 6mm and **end the stack (photo 5)**.

H. Trace a path back to the first hex. Use seven more hexes, a C, and a 6mm bead to complete a mirror image on the opposite side of the work **(photo 6)**.

Part 2

A. Cut three 4" pieces of soutache, one each of duck, rainbow metallic, and peacock. Align and stack in that order. **Prepare the thread.**

B. Locate the center of the stack. Sew up through the stack at the rib. Working from right to left, make five shaping stitches. Pick up a bead cap and a 6mm **(photo 7)**. Sew through the stack near the knot **(photo 8)**.

C. Continue working just as you would for a lollipop, treating the bead cap and bead assembly as one bead.

D. Repeat steps A–C twice to make a total of three lollipops **(photo 9)**.

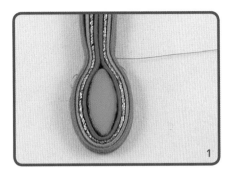

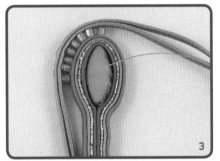

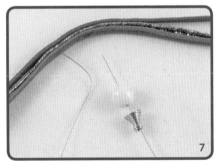

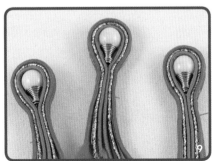

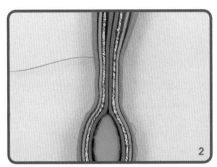

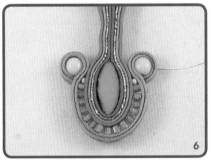

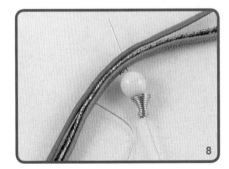

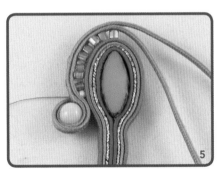

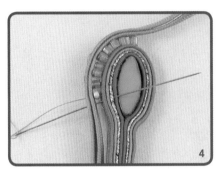

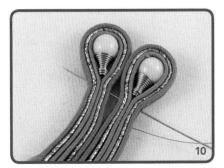

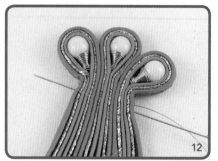

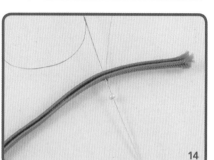

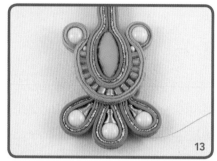

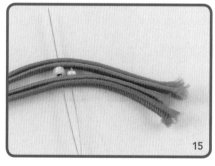

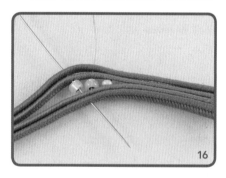

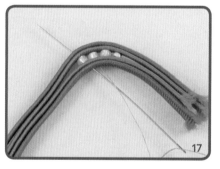

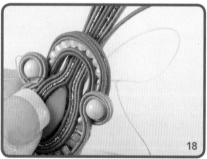

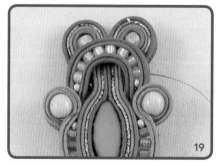

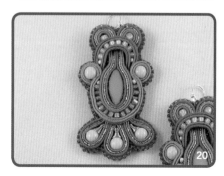

Place two lollipops side by side, and sew through the joins (**photo 10, p. 69**). Retrace the thread path twice, adding tension to close.

E. Sew through the join of the third lollipop (**photo 11**). Sew back through all three joins twice, adding tension to close the connections. Sew through the large stack three times about ¾" beyond the join to secure it (**photo 12**). Trim the ends.

F. Position Part 2 behind Part 1 and secure with **tacking stitches (photo 13)**.

Part 3 (the buckle)

A. Cut four 8" pieces of soutache, two each of peacock and duck. Align and stack a piece of peacock and duck. Sew up through the stack approximately 1½" from the right end of the stack. Sew back down through the stack and pick up a C (**photo 14**).

B. Align and stack a piece of peacock and duck. Sew down through the stack about 1½" from the right end of the stack. Sew up through the bottom stack one bead width away from where the thread last exited. Pick up a color B 8º seed bead, and sew through the upper stack (**photo 15**).

C. Continue making a ladder between the two stacks, curving the soutache as you work. Notice that the stitches on top of the ladder (**photo 16**) are longer than the stitches below it (**photo 17**); the stitches appear to go in on an angle. The longer the upper stitch is in comparison to the lower stitch, the more dramatic the curve.

D. Continue until you have incorporated eight 8ºs and another 11º. **Trim the ends.**

E. Position the halo over the top of the work, with the trimmed ends tucked behind the 6mms. Use **tacking stitches** to secure (**photo 18**).

F. Trace a path so the thread is exiting the side of the large stack above the buckle. Split the large stack in half. Add and wrap a 6º on each side of the split. **End the stacks (photo 19)**.

G. Add a jump ring at the split.

H. Apply the backing and **trim**. **Edge-bead** with color D 11º seed beads (**photo 20**).

I. Make a second earring. Add an earring finding to each jump ring.

ROSE WINDOW
choker

TOOLS

size 10 beading needle (or darning needle)

size 12 beading needle

scissors

flush cutters

flatnose pliers

MATERIALS

2 yd. ⅛" domestic soutache in each of three colors (dark lilac, poinsettia, and goldenrod)

4 yd. ⅛" domestic soutache (pansy)

5 5x12mm briolettes (red with violet AB finish) (teardrop shaped beads will work fine for this project too)

5 4mm bicone crystals (Swarovski, ruby AB)

8⁰ seed beads

- 4g color A (hybrid luster opaque Picasso)
- **17** color B (opaque curry)

3g 11⁰ seed beads (light amethyst color-lined magenta)

.5g 15⁰ (Montana blue-lined crystal AB)

2 6mm soldered jump rings (gunmetal)

6 2" 21-gauge headpins (black)

toggle clasp (black finish)

4x4" piece of Ultrasuede (scoundrel)

Nymo thread, size B (royal blue)

washable fabric glue

The challenge of the pendant for this choker lies in trying to make five long, curved ladders as close to identical as possible. The fun, however, of weaving them one over the other to make this Celtic-knot inspired piece will make it well worth your effort. As added incentive, you will then be able to fill your window with fine veining and Swarovski crystals—like leading and stained glass!

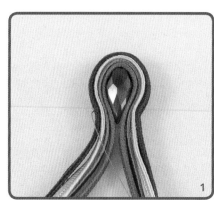

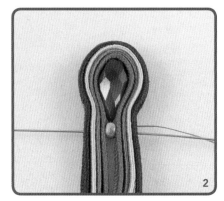

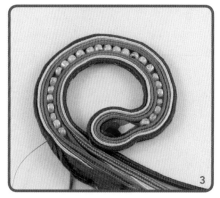

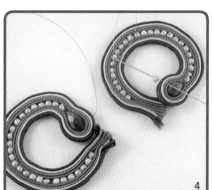

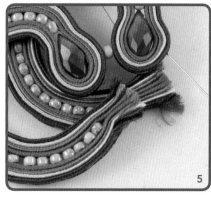

Component 1

A. Prepare the thread. Cut four 12" pieces of soutache, one of each color. **Align and stack** in this order: pansy, poinsettia, goldenrod, and dark lilac. Locate the center of the stack. Sew up through the stack 1" to the right of the center. Working from right to left, make five **shaping stitches**.

B. Sew through the briolette. Wrap the secured stack around the wide end of the briolette, and sew through the stack where the hole of bead naturally meets the stack. Retrace the thread path to secure **(photo 1)**. (If you are using a teardrop bead, treat it as you would to make a lollipop.)

C. Do not make a two-sided join. Rather, sew through one stack, pick up a color A 8º seed bead, and sew through the opposite stack **(photo 2)**.

D. Make a curved ladder using 26 As **(photo 3)**. (Try to keep your curve as smooth as possible. The opening should be roughly the size of a quarter.)

E. Repeat steps A–D four times to create a total of five elements. Try to make your elements as alike as possible.

F. Bury the knot in the front of the work, allowing the thread to exit to the right side of the briolette. Pick up a color B 8º seed bead, and sew through the left side of the next element **(photos 4, 5)**. Sew under the briolette and out of the stack on the opposite side.

G. Repeat step F until all five elements are strung together.

H. Pick up a B. Sew through the left side of the first element **(photo 6)**; the elements should now lie in a loose circle. Carefully pull the tail of each element out from the back and insert it into the loop of the element to its left **(photo 7)**. The elements should now appear to be woven together.

I. Use **tacking stitches** to secure each tail behind the briolette of the second element to the left **(photo 8)**.

J. Use tacking stitches to secure each place where one loop crosses another **(photo 9, 10)**. Working from the back, carefully trim away each tail end. Be sure that no tail ends show through the hole at the center of the work.

K. Apply backing, let dry completely, and trim. **Edge-bead** using 11º seed beads **(photo 11)**.

L. Use a darning needle to punch a hole through each opening. Insert the point of a small scissors into each hole, and carefully snip the backing away from the opening **(photo 12)**. Edge-bead inside each opening using 11º s.

M. Cut two 24" pieces of soutache in pansy. Fold one piece in half, and insert the folded end through one of the top openings **(photo 13)**. Pass the soutache ends through the loop, and pull through to make a lark's head knot **(photo 14)**. Repeat on the other side.

Veining

A. Prepare the thread. Bury the knot in the front of the work so the thread is exiting the edge beading inside one of the openings. Pick up three 15º s, a 4mm bicone, and three or four 15º s. Sew across the opening and into the edge beading on the other side **(photo 15, p. 74)**. **Retrace the thread path** so the thread is exiting the edge beading where the veining is connected, and sew just past the bicone **(photo 16, p. 74)**.

B. Pick up two or three more 15º s, and sew through the edge beading in a different spot **(photo 17, p. 74)**. Continue making randomly placed connections so the lines of beads in the opening resemble the veining on a leaf or the wing of an insect.

C. Repeat steps A and B for all openings.

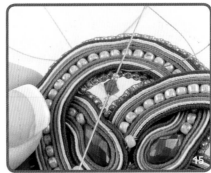

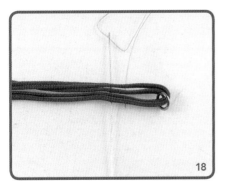

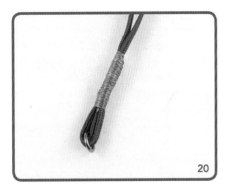

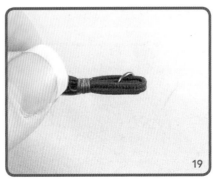

Finishing

Think about how long you want your necklace straps to be. I wanted my finished necklace to be a choker, so I made each strap (with the toggle) about 8" long. I also like to have some adjustability in my pieces, so of that 8", approximately 2" is bead chain that I can shorten or lengthen as desired. That leaves me with 6".

A. Prepare the thread. On one of the strand pairs (coming off the lark's head knot), string a jump ring until it is 6" away from the pendant. Fold the stack over the jump ring. Using a contrasting color of thread, sew up through the large stack about ¾" away from the jump ring. Working from right to left, make two or three shaping stitches to secure the large stack together for a length of about ¾" away from the knot **(photo 18)**.

B. Begin wrapping the thread tightly around the stack, covering the stitched-together area **(photo 19)**. Periodically, sew through the wrap to secure the thread, and keep wrapping.

C. Trim the loose ends of the stack, and wrap and stitch to cover the cut ends **(photo 20)**.

D. Repeat steps A–C for the other strand pair.

E. Use six headpins, six bicones, and 12 Bs to make six **bead chain links** as shown **(photo 21)**. Connect two three-link bead chains, and connect half of a toggle clasp on each end **(photo 22)**.

F. Attach the bead chain assemblies to the jump rings on each strand pair.

LADY JOSEPHINE bracelet

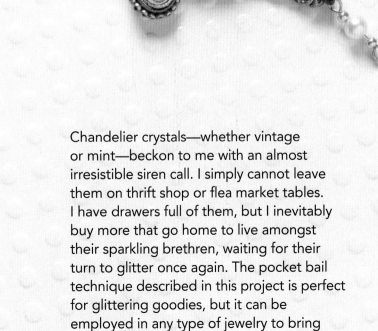

TOOLS

size 10 beading needle
scissors
flush cutters
flatnose pliers
looping pliers

MATERIALS

2 yd. ⅛" domestic soutache in each of four colors
   (marine, ivy, cream, and textured matte gold)

40x25mm chandelier crystal (green)

10x17mm Lac Jewelry element (turquoise
   and gold)

10x12mm Lac Jewelry element (turquoise
   and gold)

2 6mm glass pearls (cream)

2 4mm bicone crystals (Swarovski, indicolite AB)

4 4mm glass pearls (cream)

2 3mm glass pearls (cream)

2 6º seed beads (metallic antique gold matte)

60 8º seed beads (metallic gold)

30 10º hex beads (metallic rainbow gold/violet)

11º seed beads
   • 2g color A (metallic antique gold matte)
   • 1g color B (rainbow light topaz/sea foam
      lined)

2 6mm soldered jump rings (antique brass)

6 2" 21-gauge headpins (brass)

6mm magnetic clasp (gold-plate)

Nymo thread, size B (turquoise)

2x3" piece of beading foundation (Beadwright,
   Nicoles BeadBacking, powder blue)

4x4" piece of Ultrasuede (fern)

washable fabric glue

*Lac Jewelry components are wax-filled, foil, and
enamel beads.*

Chandelier crystals—whether vintage
or mint—beckon to me with an almost
irresistible siren call. I simply cannot leave
them on thrift shop or flea market tables.
I have drawers full of them, but I inevitably
buy more that go home to live amongst
their sparkling brethren, waiting for their
turn to glitter once again. The pocket bail
technique described in this project is perfect
for glittering goodies, but it can be
employed in any type of jewelry to bring
light and translucence to a piece.

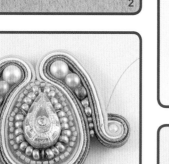

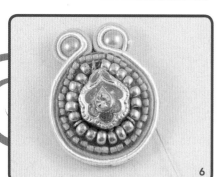

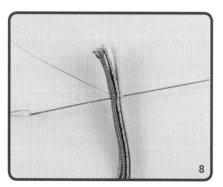

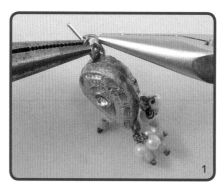

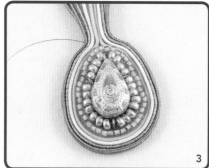

Component

A. Use pliers to carefully disassemble the Lac jewelry element and chandelier crystal, if needed **(photo 1)**.

B. Prepare the thread. Sew the larger Lac element to the beading foundation. Use 8º seed beads to surround the element with **backstitch**, and then surround the work with color B 11º seed beads **(photo 2)**.

C. Repeat step B for the smaller Lac element, and trim away the beading foundation for both.

D. Cut four 12" pieces of soutache, one of each color. **Align and stack** in this order: marine, cream, textured matte gold, and ivy. Apply the stack to the edge of the beading foundation and the larger Lac element (see p. 42) **(photo 3)**.

E. Separate the large stack. Following the layout in photo 4, use a 6mm bead, a 4mm bead, a 6º seed bead, two 8ºs, and three color A 11ºs to make a ladder on each side of the join. Add a 3mm glass pearl, wrap, and **end each stack (photo 4)**.

F. Use an A, a 4mm bicone, and an A to create a bridge at the join **(photo 5)**.

G. Cut two 8" pieces of soutache, one each of marine and cream. Align and stack in that order. Apply the stack to the edge of the beading foundation and the small Lac element. Separate the stack at the join. Add a 4mm on either side of the join, wrap, and end the stacks **(photo 6)**. Use an A, a bicone and an A to create a bridge at the join.

H. Cut two 8" pieces of soutache, one each of textured matte gold and ivy. Using hex beads, create a halo around the work (p. 49). Pull the stacks behind the work and end the stacks **(photo 7)**.

Braided loops

A. Prepare the thread. Cut three 12" pieces of soutache, one each of marine, textured matte gold, and ivy. Align and stack in that order. Sew through the stack 1" from the end. Sew through the stack three or four times at the same location to secure **(photo 8)**.

B. Braid the three pieces of soutache together **(photo 9)**. Sew the ends together to secure.

C. String two jump rings on the braid. Locate the center of the braid. Sew through the braid ¼" to the right of the center. Wrap with thread, sewing through the wrap periodically to secure. Repeat ¼" to the left of the center **(photo 10)**.

D. Keeping one jump ring to the right and the other to the left, cut the braid in half. Fold each braid assembly in half **(photo 11)**.

E. Position one braid assembly behind one of the Lac components, and use **tacking stitches** to secure **(photo 12)**. Repeat with the second braid assembly and component.

F. Apply backing to each component, but only apply glue to the half of each component that is closest to the braided loop **(photo 13)**. Trim the backing.

G. Fit the hole-end of the chandelier crystal in the pocket formed between the work and the Ultrasuede of the smaller component **(photo 14)**. Sew through the crystal's hole and use tacking stitches to secure it to the work.

H. Add a dab of glue to the back of the crystal and the underside of the Ultrasuede **(photo 15)**. Let dry completely.

I. Use As to **edge-bead** the component. Edge-bead the back of the work behind the braid assembly and crystal **(photo 16)**, and edge-bead the second component, leaving the lower portion open **(photo 17)**. Test-fit the wide end of the crystal in the pocket formed between the work

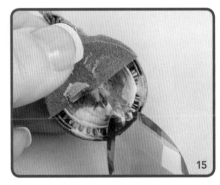

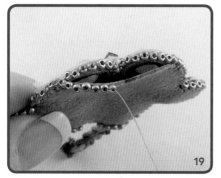

and the Ultrasuede of the second component **(photo 18)**. Edge-bead the work (the front of the pocket) separately from the Ultrasuede (the back of the pocket) **(photo 19)**.

J. Put a small dab of glue inside the pocket. Set the large end of the crystal into the pocket and let dry completely **(photo 20)**. Trace a path so the thread is exiting the edge beading where shown **(photo 21)**.

K. Pick up three As, an 8º, a 4mm, an 8º, and six As. Sew through the other component where shown **(photo 22)**. Sew down through the adjacent edge bead, pick up the same series of beads, and sew through the lower component where shown **(photo 23)**.

L. Use two headpins, two 4mm pearls, and four 8ºs to create two **bead links** as shown **(photo 24)**. Attach each link to half of a magnetic clasp (make additional links with crystals and seed beads, if desired, for length) **(photo 25)**.

M. Attach the loops on opposite ends of the links to the jump rings on the bracelet.

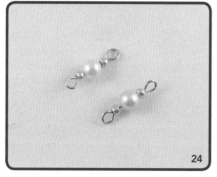

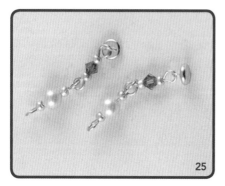

BLISSFUL ABUNDANCE necklace

MATERIALS

⅛" imported soutache

- 3 yd. in each of three colors (charcoal, sable, and garden rose)
- 1 yd. metallic bronze
- 12" scrap soutache, any color

3" rhinestone chain (pink with gold plate)

10x10mm window glass bead (lavender/pink) with Picasso edges

8mm rice-shaped freshwater pearl (dusty rose)

3 9x6mm teardrop-shaped glass pearls (cocoa)

10x6mm fire-polished flat teardrop glass bead (violet)

2 6mm glass pearls (rose)

6mm glass pearl (burgundy)

3 6mm faceted fire-polished beads (hematite)

4 assorted 6mm coordinating beads (crystal, glass, bicones, crow beads)

4mm faceted fire-polished bead (hematite)

2 4mm glass pearls (rose)

2 7x3mm wood disks (pink)

#3 (¼") bugle beads

- **3** color E (lavender gray)
- **3** color F (metallic purple)

6º seed beads

- **7–10** color A (pink metallic)
- **3–5** color B (gilt-lined medium lilac opal)

8º seed beads

- **30** color C (raspberry bronze)
- **30** color D (gilt-lined antique purple opal)

3g 11º seed beads (silver-lined champagne)

8 6mm soldered jump rings (antique brass)

12 2" 21-gauge headpins (antique brass)

toggle clasp (antique brass)

Nymo thread, size B (burgundy)

5x5" piece of Ultrasuede (violine)

2½x2½" piece of beading foundation

washable fabric glue

TOOLS

- size 10 beading needle
- scissors
- flush cutters
- flatnose pliers
- looping pliers
- permanent marker (purple)

Incorporating multiple techniques into a single piece increases the perception of complexity and detail and adds to the level of interest. If you've been making pieces that look too much alike, try this exercise and create something that uses as many different techniques as you know.

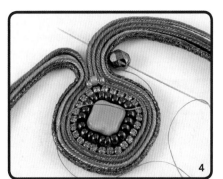

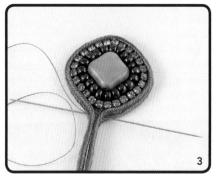

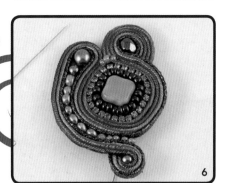

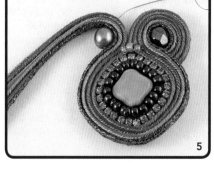

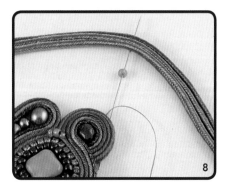

Component 1

A. Prepare the thread. Use a permanent marker to color the square of beading foundation.

B. Secure a square bead to the beading foundation (p. 42). Using color C 8º seed beads, surround the flat bead with **backstitch (photo 1)**. Surround the Cs with rhinestone chain (p. 58) **(photo 2)**. **End the thread**, and trim away the beading foundation.

C. Cut four 15" pieces of soutache, one of each color. Working from the back, apply garden rose soutache to the edge of the beading foundation (p. 42) **(photo 3)**.

D. Align and stack the remaining three 15" pieces of soutache in this order: charcoal, sable, and metallic bronze. Apply to the edge of the work.

E. Using an 11º seed bead, a color D 8º seed bead, and an 11º, **create a bridge** at the join.

F. Begin an asymmetrical split: Rotate the work and separate the strands into two stacks, moving the two innermost strands to the right. The thread should be exiting to the right of the join. Add a 6mm hematite bead **(photo 4)**. Wrap and end the stack.

G. Trace a path so the thread is exiting to the left of the join. Beginning with a 6mm bead **(photo 5)** and progressing to a 4mm bead, seven 6º color A seed beads, a D, and five 11ºs, create an open, graduated ladder with the left-hand stack. End the stack **(photo 6)**. Add and wrap a 4mm bead.

H. Trace a path so the thread is exiting the top of the stack wrapping the 6mm hematite bead **(photo 7)**. Pick up a D.

I. Cut three 6" pieces of soutache, two of sable and one of garden rose. Align and stack in that order. Locate the center of the stack, and sew through the stack at the rib.

J. Working first from left to right, use Ds to make a halo (p. 49) around the stack surrounding the 6mm **(photos 8, 9)**. End the stack. Pull the thread across the back of the work, and complete the halo in the opposite direction.

K. Cut three 4" pieces of soutache, one in each of metallic bronze, charcoal, and sable. Align and stack in that order. Sew through the stack. Wrap a 9mm teardrop bead to make a lollipop **(photo 10)**. Trim the soutache ends. Repeat this step to make another lollipop.

L. Position one lollipop behind the work and use tacking stitches to secure. Repeat with the second lollipop **(photo 11)**.

M. Cut two 8" pieces of soutache, one of metallic bronze and one of garden rose. Align and stack in that order. Use three color E bugle beads to make a parallelogram (p. 55) **(photos 12, 13)**.

N. Use shaping stitches to secure the four-strand stack into the open loop (p. 63) **(photo 14)**.

O. Repeat steps M and N, substituting charcoal soutache for the garden rose and using color F bugle beads. Position the open loops behind and over the work as shown. Use tacking stitches to secure. Trim. Add jump rings as shown **(photo 15)**.

Component 2

A. Cut four 6" pieces of soutache, one of each color. Align and stack in this order: garden rose, charcoal, sable, and metallic bronze. Using a teardrop-shaped pearl as the center, a wood disk, and a freshwater pearl, make a koala face (p. 22) with an asymmetrical split.

B. Use two 11°s and Ds to create a bridge at the join. Add a jump ring at the upper right corner of the teardrop **(photo 16)**.

Finishing

A. Apply backing to both components. Trim the backing.

B. Edge-bead using 11°s.

Make soutache-wrapped straps with open-weave beading

A. Cut two pieces of soutache (one each of sable and charcoal) four times longer than the desired strap length. Align and stack in that order. Slide four 6mm jump rings onto the stack **(photo 17)**.

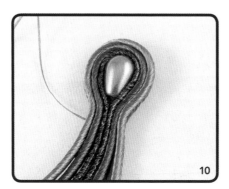

10

12

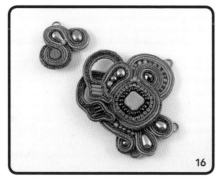

14

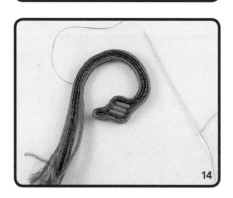

16

11

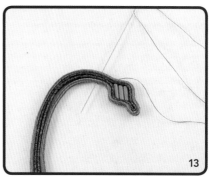

13

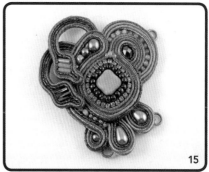

15

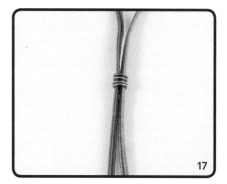

17

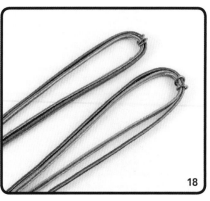

18

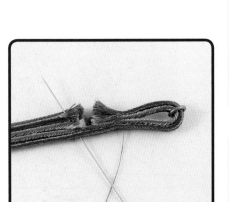

19

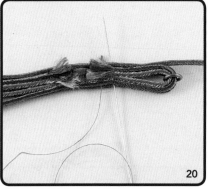

20

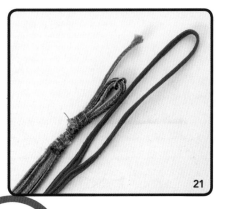

21

22

23

24

25

B. Separate the jump rings so there are two on both ends of the stack **(photo 18)**. Cut the stack in half.

C. Slide one jump ring toward one end of one stack. Fold the stack over the jump ring, and sew to secure it about 1" away from the jump ring. Fold the other end of the stack over the second jump ring. Sew the second end of the stack to meet the first end **(photo 19)**. (Dab glue on the ends, if desired.)

D. Cut a 15" length of garden rose soutache. Sew over the join, leaving a 2" tail on one side **(photo 20)**. Use thread to gently wrap the 2" section of the stack. Keep the thickness around the join as even as possible. Sew through the stack to secure.

E. Cut a 12" length of scrap soutache, and fold it in half. (This is a working loop, and it will not be incorporated into the project permanently.) Lay the soutache along the side join with the loop pointed toward the jump ring in the smaller fold **(photo 21)**. Grasp the stack and working loop in one hand. Begin to wrap the stack and the working loop with the longer end of the contrasting length of soutache **(photo 22)**.

F. Finish wrapping (about 9–10 wraps), and thread the remaining length of contrasting soutache through the working loop **(photo 23)**. Keeping a firm grasp on the wrapped section, pull the working loop through the wrap **(photo 24)**. Trim both ends of the wrap.

G. Prepare the thread. Sew through the wrap near the jump ring, and pick up 16 11ºs. Wrap the strand of beads around the end of the soutache-wrapped section. Sew through the first 11º **(photo 25)**. Sew through the soutache to secure the position of the beaded ring **(photo 26)**.

H. Sew through any bead in the ring. Pick up seven 11ºs, and sew through the fourth bead from the first **(photo 27)**. Repeat three times **(photo 28)**.

I. Sew through the first four beads of the first loop so the thread is exiting the center bead. Pick up seven 11ºs, and sew through the center bead of the adjacent loop **(photo 29)**.

Continue this pattern around to complete the round.

J. Exit the center bead of the first loop created in the previous step. Pick up seven 11ºs, and sew through the center 11ºs in the next loop. Continue this pattern around to complete the round.

K. Sew through the beads to exit the center bead in the first loop created in the previous step. Pick up three 11ºs, and sew through the next center 11º in the following loop. Repeat to complete the second circle of 11ºs around the wrapped soutache **(photo 30)**.

L. Sew through the soutache base in several places to secure, and trim the thread.

M. Repeat steps A–L to create a second strap.

Assembly

A. Prepare the thread. Sew Components 1 and 2 together as shown **(photo 31)**. Use spacer beads to adjust the fit. Be sure to **retrace the thread path** at least twice for each connection.

B. Use headpins and the remaining beads to make a dangle and eight or nine **bead chain links**. Connect the links, and attach the dangle and bead chain to jump rings. Add half of a clasp to each link at the top of the soutache-wrapped straps **(photo 32)**.

Keep your color palette consistent, and your work will look unified. At this point, you should be taking off a bit. I've given you materials, but don't fret if you don't have exactly what's on the list; use what you've got and allow your design eye to direct your decisions.

26

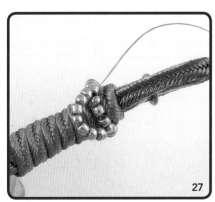

27

28

29

30

31

32

CHAIN, CHAIN, CHAIN necklace

TOOLS

size 10 beading needle
scissors
flush cutters
flatnose pliers
looping pliers
permanent marker (aqua)

MATERIALS

⅛" domestic soutache
  • 2 yd. in each of four colors (tyrol, sage, duck, and ivy)
  • 4 yd. (textured metallic matte gold)

7 10mm coin beads (cocoa pearl)

6 8x5mm fire-polished, faceted barrel-shaped beads (red AB)

27 #3 (¼") bugle beads (red)

6º seed beads
  • 6 color A (matte antique gold)
  • 6 color B (silver-lined red)

7g 8º seed beads (metallic gold)

4g 11º seed beads (metallic pearl sage)

15" 2mm (6.5ss) Swarovski crystal rhinestone chain (silk with gold plate)

7 6mm soldered jump rings (antique brass)

11 2" 21-gauge headpins (antique brass)

toggle clasp (antique brass)

Nymo thread, size B (turquoise)

5x5" piece of Ultrasuede (verde)

4½x2" piece of beading foundation

washable fabric glue

Large breastplate or bib-style necklaces can be dramatic and eye-catching. Learning to create soutache pieces that move and bend like more traditional, linked jewelry, however, is a worthy challenge. This piece is made of individual, connected links resulting in an elegant necklace that drapes beautifully and moves with the wearer.

Make larger links

A. Prepare the thread. Prepare the beading foundation by coloring it with a permanent marker.

B. Glue one of the 10mm coin beads onto the beading foundation. Let dry completely. Secure the coin to the foundation by sewing up through the foundation, through the bead, and down through the foundation three or four times **(photo 1)**. Keep the stitches close to the bead.

C. Wrap the coin with a length of rhinestone chain (p. 58). Trim the beading foundation, being careful not to cut the stitches **(photo 2)**.

D. Cut three 10" pieces of soutache, one each of sage, metallic matte gold, and tyrol. Beginning with the sage, followed by the metallic and the tyrol, secure a stack around the beading foundation (p. 42) **(photos 3, 4)**. (Hint: Let the open place in the rhinestone chain become the top part of the lollipop shape—this spot will be hidden at the end of the project.)

E. Secure an 8° seed bead between the two stacks where they meet below the center bead **(photo 5)**. **Retrace the thread path**.

F. Turn the work over. Working from the back, begin creating a curved ladder between the two stacks: Sew up through the bottom stack, pick up an 8°, and sew through the top stack **(photo 6)**. To create a consistent, smooth curve, increase the stitch length on the upper stack so the needle exits the bottom of the upper stack one and a half beads width away from the side of the previous bead. After picking up the 8°, the needle should enter the bottom stack half a bead width away from the side of the previous bead.

G. Sewing back up through the bottom stack, use the half a bead width measurement again. Pick up an 8°, and sew through the upper

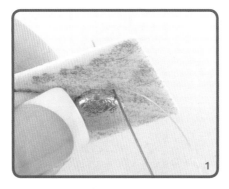

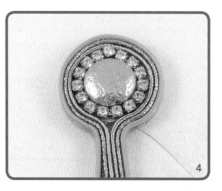

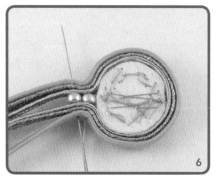

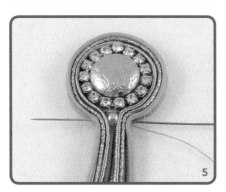

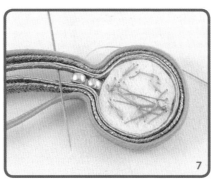

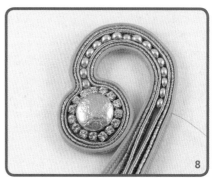

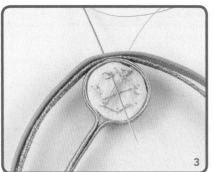

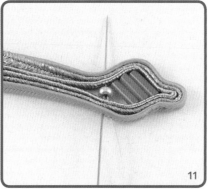

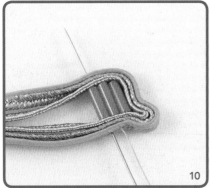

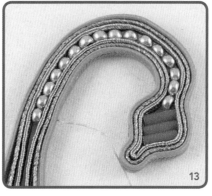

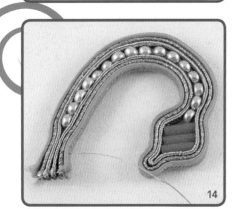

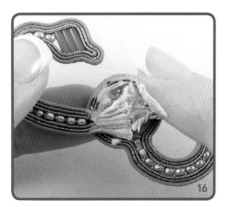

stack so the needle enters the stack one and a half bead widths away from the side of the previous bead **(photo 7, p. 85)**. Continue in this pattern, paying careful attention to the needle exit and insertion positions, until you have 16 beads incorporated into the ladder **(photo 8, p. 85)**.

H. Sew the stacks together at the end of the ladder. Trim the stacks. Use **tacking stitches** to secure the end of the ladder behind the work **(photo 9)**.

I. Cut three 8" pieces of soutache from the same colors, one of each color. **Align and stack** the pieces in the same order as the stack surrounding the coin bead. Locate the center of the stack, and sew up through the stack. Using three bugle beads, begin making a parallelogram (see p. 56) **(photo 10)**. At the point where you would normally join the two stacks near the top of the work, secure an 8° between the two stacks **(photo 11)**.

J. Working from the front, begin creating a curved ladder between the two stacks. Use the same spacing described in steps E–G until you have eight beads incorporated into the curve **(photo 12)**.

K. Continue making the ladder, incorporating eight more beads, but flatten the curve by changing the stitch length on the upper curve to three-fourths bead width **(photo 13)**. Sew the stacks together and trim **(photo 14)**.

L. Position the parallelogram behind the first component so the parallelogram appears to be a natural extension of the first component's curved ladder. Use **tacking stitches** to secure the second component behind the first **(photo 15)**.

M. Cut a 1¼x1¼" piece of Ultrasuede. Apply a dab of glue to the center back of the work only. Use your finger or a toothpick to spread glue thinly across the back (don't let the glue get on the ladders) **(photo 16)**.

N. Apply the backing. Let dry completely, and then **trim the backing**. Under the ladders, follow the shape of the round center.

O. Edge-bead. Where the Ultrasuede edge passes under the ladders, edge-bead the edge of the Ultrasuede only **(photo 17)**. Bury the thread.

P. Using ivy, textured matte gold, and duck soutache, repeat steps A–O. **Add a jump ring** at the bottom of the link, and then continue to follow steps A–O **(photo 18)**.

Q. Push the parallelogram of link 1 through the left-hand loop of link 2 **(photo 19)**. Use **tacking stitches** to secure the tip of the parallelogram of link 1 over the stack, wrapping the center of the link **(photo 20)**. Make the tacking stitches on the back of the work very small, and they will disappear into the Ultrasuede.

R. Alternating between the two color combinations of soutache, make and connect five more links. Add jump rings to links 3, 4, 5, and 6 only **(photo 21)**.

Make smaller links

A. Cut six 8" pieces of soutache, two each of ivy, textured matte gold, and duck. Using three bugle beads and 16 8°s each, make two identical parallelograms with curved ladders **(photo 22)**.

B. Flip the right one over to make a mirrored pair.

C. Add a jump ring behind the "beak" of each parallelogram **(photo 23)**. Use tacking stitches to secure the ladder of the right-hand smaller link behind the parallelogram.

D. Apply a dab of glue behind only the parallelogram that has its ladder secured behind it. Use your fingertip or a toothpick to spread the glue so it covers the back of the parallelogram portion of the smaller link *only*.

E. Apply the backing, and let dry completely. **Trim the backing. Edge-bead** using 11°s **(photo 24)**.

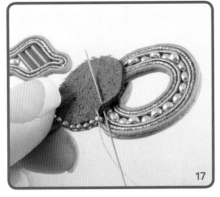

17

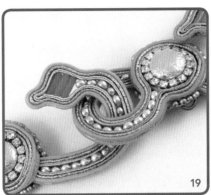

19

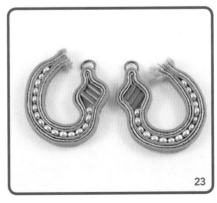

21

18

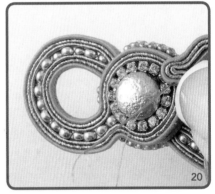

20

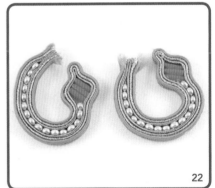

22

24

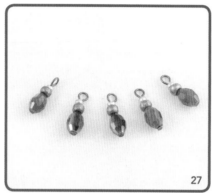

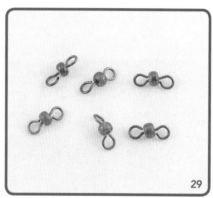

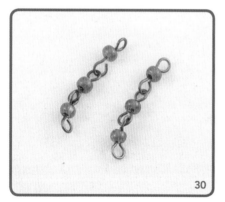

F. Push the parallelogram of link 7 through the loop of the right-hand smaller link **(photo 25)**. Use tacking stitches to secure the parallelogram of link 7 over the stack wrapping the coin bead of the same link.

G. Push the left-hand smaller link through the back of the left-hand loop of link 1 **(photo 26)**. Use tacking stitches to secure the ladder of the left-hand smaller link behind the parallelogram. Apply backing and edge-bead as in steps D and E.

Finishing

A. Using five headpins, five faceted beads, five color A 6° seed beads, and five 8°s, make five **dangles (photo 27)**. Attach a loop on one dangle to the jump ring on link 2 **(photo 28)**. Attach the remaining four dangles to the other links.

B. Using six headpins and six color B 6°s, make six **bead chain links (photo 29)**. Make two chains with three bead chain links each **(photo 30)**.

C. Attach half of a clasp to the end of each chain. Attach the bead chain/clasp assemblies to the jump rings and ends of the linked work **(photo 31)**.

"Cleopatra's Cavalry" cuff bracelet, 2010

"Blossom Pendant for Anu" necklace, 2013

"Ebb & Flow" necklace, 2010

"My Heart's Labyrinth" necklace, 2013

"In Living Color" soft cuff, 2013

"Dangerous Liaisons" necklace, 2013

"Breakfast at Tiffany's" earrings, 2013

"Bollywood Wedding" earrings, 2012

"Roses Released from the Tapestry" necklace, 2013 Bead Dreams Finalist

"Raiment for Anu" necklace, 2013

"Something Blue" necklace, 2012

"Zeal" cuff, 2012

"Night at the Opera" earrings, 2012

"Caribbean Queen" necklace, 2013 (polymer clay cabochons, beads, and toggle by Ann Dillon)

"Caryn's Fifi Necklace" 2012

"Mirth" cuff, 2011

Resources

Beads, findings, supplies, soutache, and Ultrasuede
Amee Runs with Scissors
488 Hanover St. Apt. 1 Manchester, NH 03104
603-759-0083, ameerunswithscissors.com

Beads, findings, and supplies
Ann Dillon (polymer clay beads and cabochons)
anndillon.com

Cherry Tree Beads (wholesale)
95 Thompson St. Unit 125, Asheville, NC 28803
828-505-2328, order@cherrytreebeads.com

Designer's Findings
P.O. Box 1433 Brookfield, WI 53008
262.574.1324, designersfindings@wi.rr.com

Fusion Beads
3830 Stone Way N Seattle, WA 98103
888-781-3559, fusionbeads.com

Margola (wholesale)
232 South Van Brunt St. Englewood, NJ 07631
201-816-9500, margola.com

Whimbeads
121 E. Cotati Ave. Cotati, CA US 94931
800-232-111, whimbeads.com

Thaya Collections LLC (owner, Thaya Salamacha; Lac Jewelry) thayasa@hotmail.com

Soutache
BeadSmith/Helby Import Co. (wholesale only)
37 Hayward Ave. Carteret, NJ 07008
732-969-5300, info@helby.com

Ultrasuede
Field's Fabrics
3975 Lake Michigan Drive NW
Grand Rapids, MI 49534
800.678.5872, fieldsfabrics.com

Acknowledgments

Mae Rockland-Tupa and Victoria Tane: You are the generous beacons who shed your brilliant light on the fact that within the most successful of craftswomen, the soul of the artist and the brain of the business woman must be inextricably linked.

Caryn, my heart's sister: You are ever my model for femininity without fragility.

Julia Gerlach, editor of *Bead&Button* magazine: Thank you for finding me.

Jane Cruz, associate editor of *Bead&Button*: Thank you for your patience and unflagging enthusiasm.

Dianne Wheeler, editor-in-chief of Kalmbach Books: Thank you for granting me, fairy-godmother-style, this most precious of opportunities.

Erica Swanson, associate editor of Kalmbach Books: Thank you for your professionalism, perseverance, and positivity.

Tom Ford, art director, and James Forbes, photographer: "Clean," I said. "Bright," I said. "Exciting," I said. You listened. You responded. And then you made it better than anything I ever imagined.

About the Author

When people ask me, "Why is your art business called Amee Runs with Scissors?" I usually just laugh and say, "Because it sounds a whole lot sexier than 'Amee Eats Paste.'"

You see, my creative spirit seems to be about as predictable as a sugared-up six-year-old. But I have come to trust this wild-eyed, slightly-manic inner child because she might just whisper something really inspiring like, "Hey! Let's put some Ultrasuede in the Sizzix machine!"

I have worked as professional interior designer for over 25 years but, in my thirties, I went back to school to pursue a degree in fine art. Somewhere along the way, I discovered soutache and bead embroidery. I am a proud member of the League of New Hampshire Craftsmen and have been fortunate enough to have had my work published on the cover of *Bead&Button* magazine. I work out of my home in southern New Hampshire, making one-of-a-kind pieces of wearable-art textile-jewelry. I write, sell soutache and bead embroidery supplies, and teach classes out of my studio and at venues across the country.

Photo by Photography by Nylora, Concord, NH

Embark on new adventures in beading

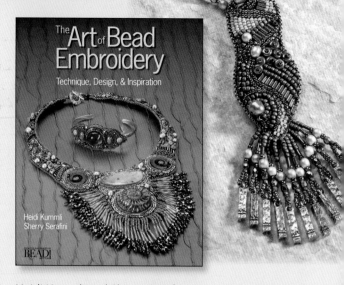
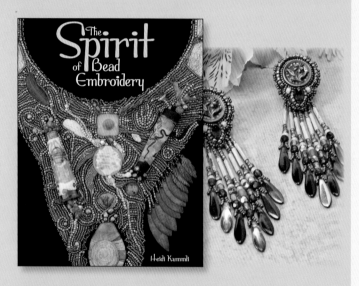

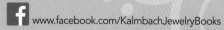